THE
LANGUAGE
OF
FLOWERS

A Fully Illustrated Compendium
of Meaning, Literature, and Lore
for the Modern Romantic

• ◊ • ◊ • ◊ • ◊ • ◊ • ◊ •

Written and Illustrated by

ODESSA BEGAY

HARPER
DESIGN
An Imprint of HarperCollinsPublishers

CONTENTS

• ◇ • ◇ • ◇ • ◇ •

INTRODUCTION

When my husband and I bought our first house a few years ago, we had a lot of work to do. There were walls to paint, windows to replace, floors to sand, and seemingly endless boxes to unpack. It seemed that there was no shortage of tasks to take on to make our indoor living space actually inhabitable. Despite all that, the first thing I did once we moved in was head to the backyard to try to make something out of the sad little patches of dirt where it seemed all hopes of a garden had been abandoned long ago.

When planning my garden, I did what most gardeners do: I considered the color, shape, and structure of the plantings, flowering and nonflowering alike—and I also thought about which ones might attract more birds and butterflies. I was overwhelmed but elated by the idea of creating an outdoor space from scratch. The possibilities seemed as endless as beginning a new drawing on a blank page. Creating an outdoor composition of plants gave me a sense of freedom—the only limitations were the climate and our property line.

If I'd been a gardener 150 years ago, I may have had another factor to consider: floriography, the practice of using flowers and floral arrangements to send coded messages. During Queen Victoria's reign, from her coronation in 1838 to her death in 1901, floriography, or the language of flowers, was a fascination that swept England and then spread worldwide.

The interest in floriography was not unique to the Victorians, but it may have been the only time the meanings of flowers were so obsessively woven into all aspects of the sociocultural environment. For thousands of years and across civilizations, flowers have held one significance or another in literature, the decorative arts, religion, and economics. Certainly, flower bouquets existed long before the Victorian era, but they were created primarily for medicinal or superstitious purposes. The Victorians turned flowers and gardening into a passionate hobby. They kept extensive gardens on their properties, practiced horticulture in greenhouses, and even propagated new species. They journeyed worldwide in search of exotic plants and cultivated rare or newly found specimens in terrariums, a Victorian invention created for the purpose of transporting plants home from far-flung locations.

The history of books about floriography is also a complex one. According to Beverly Seaton's *The Language of Flowers: A History* (1995), the first known book that combined illustrations of flowers with poetry about them was *Guirlande de Julie* (Garland for Julie), which was created in 1641 by Charles de Sainte-Maure, the Duke of Montausier, who was also the tutor of King Louis XIV's eldest son, the dauphin Louis. The duke commissioned the book as a winter birthday gift for his fiancée, Julie d'Angennes, as flowers were not available during the season.

The idea of the language of flowers was first imported to Europe by the English aristocrat and poet Lady Mary Wortley Montagu via letters. While traveling in Turkey in 1717 and 1718, she wrote to her family and friends in England, describing her journey. The letters were shared among friends, but weren't made public until 1763, one year after Montagu's death. In one of the letters to her friend Lady Rich, Montagu shares a poem that she refers to as a Turkish love letter. She writes, "There is no colour, no flower, no weed, no fruit, herb, pebble, or feather, that has not a verse belonging to it; and you may quarrel, reproach, or send letters of passion, friendship, or civility, or even of news, without ever inking your fingers." Seaton points out that Montagu was incorrectly describing sélam, a secret Turkish love language used by women in a harem to communicate with outside lovers (apparently, they would never have sent objects to one another). Despite Montagu's misinterpretation, the idea sparked an interest in sending messages via coded objects that would have meaning to the letters' recipients. Another person credited with introducing floriography to Europe was the French author and traveler Aubry de La Mottraye. In Sweden, he had published his own account of sélam in 1724, but the popularity of the trend has been more closely attributed to Montagu because of her succinctly written description. This was the beginning of floriography, but the practice was slow to develop.

Sometime between 1784 and 1818, it became common practice for men to give women books like *Guirlande de Julie* as New Year's gifts. In December 1819, the first book on the subject, *Le langage des fleurs* by Louise Cortambert was published with the likely intention of a New Year's distribution. While the book was popular, communicating via a floral vocabulary didn't become a full-blown trend until Queen Victoria married Prince Albert in 1840. During the ceremony, she carried a small bouquet of snowdrops (allegedly Albert's favorite flower) that charmed the public. The popularity of flower posies soared, both as a wedding accessory and a means of discrete communication among the members of the upper class. Queen Victoria's wedding ushered in some other lasting bridal traditions, too. Prior to her choice of a white gown, wealthy brides wore an elaborate dress—in any color—created for the occasion, while less well-off brides wore their best dress. Most royal ceremonies were conducted at night, but Victoria and Albert were married in the afternoon, resulting in a change in that custom as well.

Victorians loved romanticism and sentimentality in art and literature, but adhered to a rigid code of etiquette that disapproved of direct expression. Obvious flirtation; direct questions, particularly about relationships; and any other comments that could possibly be perceived as immodest or indiscrete were highly frowned upon. A small bouquet of flowers was a common social gift among upper society at the time, and the Victorians became inspired to assemble these floral compositions to convey their exact sentiments to the recipient in a manner appropriate to the social situation. Of course, for a messaging system to work properly, there needs to be an established set of definitions, a code that people everywhere can acknowledge, agree upon, and use. The exploding popularity of floriography made it nearly impossible to create a precise system of sorts, to assign one universal meaning to every flower. But that didn't stop the Victorians from trying.

The popularity of floriography contributed to the publication of a host of dictionaries, primarily aimed at women, cataloging the meanings of flowers. Each had a specific bent, be it literary, scientific, or recreational, and the lists of flowers and their significance varied from book to book. Some dictionaries were for pure pleasure, like Kate Greenaway's illustrated *Language of Flowers* (1884), which simply lists the flowers with their assigned meanings, then offers a selection of flower-themed poems at the back. Others, such as Henry Phillips's *Floral Emblems* (1825), attempt to give more of an explanation behind the symbology by including small pieces of tangentially related historical information or an excerpt from a poem about the flower. In Elizabeth Washington Wirt's famous *Flora's Dictionary* (1832), she combines the sentimentality of the flower list and poetic excerpts with plenty of historical notes, but rarely addresses the reasoning behind their symbols. These dictionaries contain only a few examples of coded bouquets and, according to Seaton, there doesn't seem to be any proof that this method of communicating was practiced, but rather, only discussed extensively.

The flowers mentioned in these books are rarely illustrated alongside their respective poems or annotations. As a gardener and an illustrator, I found this, and the inconsistency of interpretation, both disappointing and frustrating, so when I was asked by my editor at HarperCollins whether I might like to create a contemporary floriography dictionary, I jumped at the chance.

In creating this modern volume, I chose fifty of the most enduring and popular varieties for gardening and floral arrangements today. In researching these flowers and their symbology, I discovered an astounding amount of variance in their meanings and uses, all of which seemed to change based on date, location, and writer. I realized there was so much more to learn about the plants beyond their associations. I spent hours combing through medieval manuscripts, squinting at nearly incomprehensible Old English in spiky Gothic lettering. Look at Raphael Holinshed's *The Chronicles of England, from William the Conquerour (who began his reigne ouer this land, in the yeare after Christes natiuitie 1066) vntill the yeare 1577* (1585) or Henry Lyte's *A niewe Herball, or Historie of plantes* (1578) if you want to see what I mean. I sifted through countless antique herbal remedy and poetry books, scans of nineteenth-century newspapers and journals, and modern research papers intended for scientists only. Some of these sources shared threads of a common narrative about the flowers, while others were dubiously translated from ancient languages or presented as fact by secondhand half stories filled with details from unspecified poets. I also discovered that if an opinion exists, and one almost always does, there's probably a treatise about it. Of course, the people who wrote these ancient books and journals aren't here to answer questions, leaving the rest of us to rely on conjecture and our best guesses. Suffice it to say, there were more than a few inconsistencies among these materials.

That said, I aimed to select the information that seemed the most universally agreed upon in both art and science, or that which had the oldest available resource that could be cross-referenced with newer materials. When credible opinions and definitions varied, I point that out in this book's entries. I also aimed to select interesting stories that were unique to specific flowers. I don't think it would come as a surprise to know that there are countless books and journals dedicated solely to many of the plants and subjects in the book.

With each entry, I offer an overview of the flower's history and how its names and meanings were assigned through science, folklore, myth, and ancient medicinal uses. Some of the subjects, such as the Victorians' penchant for Orientalism or the influence of the Age of Enlightenment on Victorian ideals, are too complex to attempt to cover in detail, but I acknowledge these practices in their respective entries and make them part of the overall context of floriography. Whenever possible, I've added anecdotes, literary references, quotations, and compelling facts to provide a fuller picture of a flower's significance and place in culture. When creating illustrations for the book, I tried to match the flowers with the definitions selected based on my research.

This book is for the contemporary flower lover, but it also considers the past and future. By the 1880s attitudes toward sentimentality were changing and the popularity of the language of flowers was beginning to wane, increasingly considered an old-fashioned, gimmicky amusement. Many Victorian hobbyist gardening and bouquet-giving practices were on the decline as well. When World War I began in 1914, cultivating flowers on a grand scale ended abruptly. Greenhouses were needed for food storage and converted into victory gardens. The collective focus shifted to furthering war efforts or supporting burgeoning interests in social movements such as women's suffrage and improved working conditions. Women, particularly in England, began to make up a significant part of the industrialized workforce as men went off to war. This isn't to say that people entirely stopped caring about gardening or attending flower shows, but social and political strife along with scientific advancement seemed to break the spell once cast by horticultural beauty and discovery, and a floral code.

Happily, the beauty of flowers and the romance they inspire has stayed with us. Meanings may have been attributed to them, but they also have stories to tell. I hope reading about these flowers inspires you to try gardening, grow a fragrant flower inside, or visit some historic gardens in your area that are still flourishing today. There could even be a garden in your current city that you didn't know about. Somewhere in your life is a blank page, waiting to be filled with flowers.

THE
FLOWERS

ACACIA

Robinia pseudoacacia

PURPLE: Significance uncertain
ROSE: Friendship
WHITE: Elegance
YELLOW: Concealed or secret love

• ◊ • ◊ • ◊ • ◊ •

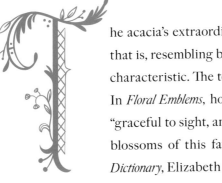he acacia's extraordinary blossoms are papilionaceous, that is, resembling butterfly wings in form, a delightful characteristic. The term was beloved by the Victorians. In *Floral Emblems*, horticulturist Henry Phillips writes, "graceful to sight, and elegant hang the papilionaceous blossoms of this favorite flowering shrub." In *Flora's Dictionary*, Elizabeth Washington Wirt fondly notes the rose acacia's "copious, large, pink-petaled, papilionaceous blossoms."

The word *acacia* comes from the Greek root *akakía*, which roughly translates as "thorny Egyptian tree." The acacia, as it's described in the Victorian language of flowers, refers to the black locust tree, which has no relation to the Australian acacia tree (also known as the wattle), although both species are known to bear long sharp spines on their branches. Of the many species of the black locust bearing spiky branches, the yellow-flowered spiny acacia (*Robinia spinosa*) native to Russia and China was often used to line the tops of outer city and village walls as a defense to keep out intruders. In *A General System of Gardening and Botany*, the nineteenth-century Scottish botanist and explorer George Don writes that in Beijing, "they [stuck] the bushes in clay on the tops of their walls, to prevent persons from getting or looking over them" and that the shrub was "well adapted to grow as impenetrable hedges, on account of its long branches and long thorns." The wood of the tree is sturdy and rot resistant. It has not only been put to great use as timber, but was also frequently used by Native Americans for making bows for hunting.

In Europe, especially in rural areas of France and Italy, acacia petals are often used in pancakes and fritters in spring, for this is when the flowers are beginning to bloom and are at their most tender and fragrant. The scent of the acacia is sweet, similar to that of honey, while its flavor varies from delicate and floral to slightly peppery. There are many recipes for these desserts to be found online, including locust-flower fritters from Jacques Pépin's book *Heart & Soul in the Kitchen*.

Acacia petals are also used to flavor simple syrups and liquors as well as to make tea. The syrup or liquor can be made by steeping the flowers in boiling water, before adding sugar, while the tea can be made with fresh or dried flowers that are then boiled or steeped in hot water. The flowers may be edible, but the remaining parts of the tree are toxic and should be avoided. Some homeopathic herbal remedies say that when boiled, the seed pods and bark can be ingested in small quantities to help with digestive issues and convulsions, but this is not advised.

• ◊ • ◊ • • ◊ •

Light-leaved acacias, by the door,
Stood up in balmy air,
Clusters of blossomed moonlight bore,
And breathed a perfume rare.

—GEORGE MACDONALD
"Songs of the Spring Nights,"
from *The Disciple, and Other Poems*, 1867

A FEAST OF FLOWERS

In *Plant Lore, Legends, and Lyrics*, Richard Folkard writes that garlands and chaplets (flower crowns) were commonly used by the ancient Egyptians to decorate themselves, their homes, and their altars. These often included anemones and chrysanthemums, and blooms from trees including acacia, olive, myrtle, and others. Folkard shares an anecdote written by Roman author, naturalist, and philosopher Pliny the Elder (AD 23–79), who says that at feasts, guests and attendants were adorned with wreaths, and homes and wine cups were adorned with flowers. It was a frequent custom for both Greeks and Romans to mix the flowers of their chaplets in their wine, then drink to the health of their friends.

One story recounts a feast held by Cleopatra and attended by Mark Antony, who, due to his fear of being poisoned, would never eat or drink at her table without his tester sampling first. Cleopatra ordered a chaplet of flowers, the edges of which were dipped in a deadly poison, to be prepared for the Roman general. Her own chaplet was mixed with aromatic spices. When the party had become lively from drink, Cleopatra raised a toast to Antony's health, took off her chaplet, rubbed the blossoms into her goblet, and drank off the contents. Antony was about to follow her example but, just as he raised the fatal cup to his lips, Cleopatra seized his arm, exclaiming, "Cure your jealous fears and learn that I should not have to seek the means of your destruction, could I live without you." Then, she ordered a prisoner to be brought before them, who, on drinking the wine from Antony's goblet, died instantly in their presence.

Mt. Fuji

AZALEA

Rhododendron

Temperance

• ◊ • ◊ • ◊ • ◊ •

In 1603, after the shogunate arrived in Edo (feudal Tokyo) with their warrior caste of samurai, trade and travel between Japan and other countries ceased. This isolation had the effect of focusing societal concentration on a specific variety of practices and solidifying their place within the Japanese cultural identity. This was especially true for floriculture, the cultivation of flowering plants primarily for their ornamental qualities. Both upper and lower classes were able to enjoy the practice. Large gardens were a symbol of prestige, so samurai, who were high-ranking members of society, began to hire farmers to create and tend to elaborate flower gardens on their properties.

During the 1600s, Ito-Ihei III of the Somei area gained prominence as a skilled gardener and nurseryman and developed his knowledge of azaleas, many of which which are native to Japan. Sometime between 1682 and 1684, he began distributing them in the surrounding area. In 1692, he wrote *Kinshumakura*, an illustrated guide to azaleas that included more than three hundred cultivars he had developed, and enhanced their popularity in Japan.

In the mid-1840s, Scottish botanist Robert Fortune first brought the azalea, in the form of seeds, to England. Fortune had been sent to China by the British East India Company to spy on the Chinese and steal their secrets to tea production and horticultural practices. He managed to smuggle home a variety of seeds and plant cuttings. Some of these other plants included the yellow rose, kumquat, winter jasmine, and wisteria.

Azalea belongs to the *Rhododendron* genus of the Ericaceae family, which includes edible plants such as blueberries, huckleberries, and cranberries. Azaleas, however, are highly toxic. In fact, they are so toxic that even the honey they produce has proved to be poisonous. In Chinese culture, azaleas are referred to as *sixiang shu*, which translates to "thinking-of-home bush," and they were often featured in the poetry of the prominent Tang dynasty poet, Du Fu (712–770).

Ornamental plants that can be grown in many colors and are easy to hybridize, azaleas became a staple of the English Victorian garden. Not only were they commonly available for purchase in an endless variety of sizes and colors through florists' catalogs, but they also appeared in some turn-of-the-century books on floral arrangement as the primary, and sometimes only, flower in Christmas and Easter flower baskets and table arrangements. In Henry Phillips's *Floral Emblems*, he writes that azaleas prefer poor, dry soil and do not fare well in the often overly fertilized soil of English gardens; therefore, they are an appropriate symbol of "temperance" for their ability to take only what they need to survive.

There is no difference between knowledge and temperance;
for he who knows what is good and embraces it, who knows
what is bad and avoids it, is learned and temperate.

—SOCRATES
Treasury of Thought: Forming an Encyclopedia of Quotations
from Ancient and Modern Authors, 1884

MISS MAUDIE'S
MOST PRIZED FLOWER

In *To Kill a Mockingbird*, Harper Lee often uses flowers symbolically. Azaleas, for example, are the sympathetic character Miss Maudie's most prized possessions. As the azalea is available in various colors, it's been said that it represents her kindness and racial tolerance, which other characters in the novel lack. Lee writes that Miss Maudie "loved everything that grew in God's earth, even the weeds."

Miss Maudie not only has many sides to her personality, like the many shades of azalea, but she also does her best to look out for those in her neighborhood and to care for her garden and herself, a symbol of temperance. Lee writes, "Miss Maudie hated her house: time spent indoors was time wasted. She was a widow, a chameleon lady who worked in her flower beds in an old straw hat and men's coveralls, but after her five o'clock bath she would appear on the porch and reign over the street in magisterial beauty."

BUTTERCUP

Ranunculus acris

Ingratitude, childishness

• ◊ • ◊ • ◊ • ◊ •

uring the Victorian era, the buttercup was popular as an easy-to-grow ground cover or garden-border filler, but there's not much evidence of wide use in bouquets. In Henry Phillips's *Floral Emblems*, he writes that, although the buttercup is a cheerful-looking addition to gardens and meadows, "it enters so frequently into the sports of infancy," which is why the flower came to symbolize childishness. A centuries-old children's game is to hold the flower of a yellow buttercup under the chin of a friend. If the chin glows bright yellow it means the person likes butter.

The buttercup's reflective ability can be attributed to a unique cellular makeup that allows the top surface of its petals to reflect yellow light with an intensity similar to glass. In addition to reflecting bright yellow light, the buttercup can reflect large amounts of UV light, which attracts pollinating insects. Alas, we must pity the poor unsuspecting bee seduced by this vibrant flower that appears to be glistening with nectar. Like the singer in "Build Me Up Buttercup," the popular 1968 song written by the British soul group the Foundations, the bee would be let down by an object of desire.

The buttercup is an ancient, wild meadow flower in the *Ranunculus* genus, which comprises more than six hundred different species. Seed fossil records of extinct varieties of ranunculus from the Pliocene Borsoni formation in the

Rhön Mountains of Germany indicate that the buttercup may be between 2.6 and 5.3 million years old. The Latin word *ranunculus* means "little frog" or *tadpole*, and like a frog, these plants are often described in medieval botanical manuscripts as being found growing near water.

While the flower of the buttercup is primarily a bright yellow color that has a shiny appearance, a handful of species occur with white, orange, red, or purple flowers. Most buttercups have solid, dark-green leaves, but some have green leaves with white spots and others have dark-purple leaves that can look almost black. Buttercups were once known in medieval Europe as king's cups because of their resemblance to a crown. In *A niewe Herball*, English botanist Henry Lyte described a black-leaved water crowfoot called "leopards claws" and a golden crowfoot that he called a "butter flower." He doesn't specifically state why it was called a butter flower, but does write of its shiny, gold, cup-shaped blossom.

Most buttercup species in the Northern Hemisphere bloom from April to May, which, according to *Flora's Dictionary*, is "the season when the best butter is made." This may be one source of the lore behind its common name. Another theory for the name—albeit a falsehood—was that buttercups, which were eaten by cows, gave butter its yellow hue. The truth is that the plant is quite toxic, with a bitter taste and the ability to cause blistering in the mouth; animals rarely eat it.

Despite its toxicity, its ability to blister skin made buttercups useful medicinally in the sixteenth century, when it was crushed and applied to growths and lesions to make them fall off. The dried and powdered root could be inhaled in small quantities to aid with sinus problems, too. Earlier, the ancient people of the Native American Nez Perce tribe consumed the roots and seeds of the buttercup after cooking and drying them as an antidote to the flower's poisonous petals, but whether this worked or not is unclear—and not an advisable remedy.

The Meadows Are Yellow with Buttercups

George Augustus Moore (1852–1933) was an Irish novelist and man of letters. Credited with paving the way for modern realism and bringing French naturalism to fiction. Because he took on real issues, including extramarital sex, prostitution, and lesbianism, his work was repeatedly banned from British circulating libraries and booksellers due to its "immorality."

Nonetheless, Moore's books were popular with the Victorians, who clearly relished reading about the multitude of subjects forbidden from conversation according to the formal etiquette of their day. His novel *A Mere Accident* (1887) tells the story of a young man well practiced in self-denial who is drawn to the church, yet he falls in love with a beautiful woman and is overcome with desire for her. The following is an excerpt from that novel that Victorians must have loved for its suggestion of stirring passion amidst a colorful spring setting—buttercups included.

CHAPTER V.

But if in the morning he were strong, Kitty was more beautiful than ever, and they walked out in the sunlight. They walked out on the green sward, under the evergreen oaks where the young rooks are swinging; out on the mundane swards into the pleasure ground; a rosery and a rockery; the pleasure ground divided from the park by iron railings, the park encircled by the rich elms, the elms shutting out the view of the lofty downs.

The meadows are yellow with buttercups, and the birds fly out of the gold. And the golden note is prolonged through the pleasure grounds by the pale yellow of the laburnums, by the great yellow of the berberis, by the cadmium yellow of the gorse, by the golden wallflowers growing amid rhododendrons and laurels. . . .

Pansies, pale yellow pansies!

The sun glinting on the foliage of the elms spreads a napery of vivid green, and the trunks come out black upon the cloth of gold, and the larks fly out of the gold, and the sky is a single sapphire, and two white clouds are floating. It is May time.

CALLA LILY

Zantedeschia aethiopica

WHITE: Feminine modesty

• ◇ • ◇ •◇• ◇ •

he calla lily is most commonly white, but is also cultivated in yellow, pink, green, orange, and a purple that is
so dark that it is almost black. In Victorian times, white
was the only color that seemed to hold any significance,
although florists today have broadly assigned joy or
gratitude to yellow, admiration to pink, and royalty or
strength to dark purple.

The name *calla lily* is misleading, as the flower is neither
a part of the calla nor the lily families. The flower belongs to the Araceae
family, a group of flowers that grow with a single spikelike spadix, a fleshy
stem covered in tiny, closely clustered flowers. The word *calla* comes from the
Greek word *kallos*, meaning "beautiful," while the word *lily* comes from the Old
English word *lilia*, which had been used during the sixteenth century as an
adjective meaning "white, pure, and lovely."

In Roman mythology, Venus was said to have been so jealous of the beauty
of the calla lily that, in an attempt to mar its appearance, she caused a huge
yellow pistil to sprout from its center. According to *Flora's Dictionary*, the calla
lily was enjoyed in Victorian gardens for its strong "agreeable" fragrance and
striking alabaster color. The combination of its elegant, vaselike shape and
bright yellow spadix often inspired Elizabeth Washington Wirt to compare
it to a "beautiful antique lamp" used for burning incense during her day. The

flower has been a popular choice for wedding bouquets and table centerpieces since that time, too. It also has been closely associated with spring, Easter, and the resurrection of Jesus, tying it to symbols of holiness, purity, and rebirth. For these reasons it has also become a traditional floral choice at funerals.

The calla lily, along with the sunflower, was a symbol of the nineteenth-century Aesthetic art movement, which placed emphasis on the appeal of visual and written art rather than any deeper symbolic meaning. Adherents "subscribed to the notion that by surrounding oneself with beautiful things one would become beautiful," according to the Art Institute of Chicago. Oscar Wilde, a prominent supporter of this movement, was known to place calla lilies and sunflowers on his dining table when entertaining.

The white calla lily was not only a favorite flower of Georgia O'Keeffe, but also one of the artist's signature subjects and the flower most closely associated with her work. Having grown up on a farm, O'Keeffe felt a deep connection to nature, especially flowers. In a letter to American photographer Anita Pollitzer, she asks, "Anita, do you feel like flowers sometimes?" Art historian Marjorie Balge-Crozier suggested in *Georgia O'Keeffe: The Poetry of Things* that the artist's close-up paintings of flowers weren't merely studies of form or potential allegories for female sexuality, but possibly self-portraits as well.

• ◊ • ◊ • ◊ • ◊ •

Can it be
That modesty may more betray our sense
Than woman's lightness? Having waste ground enough,
Shall we desire to raze the sanctuary
And pitch our evils there?

—WILLIAM SHAKESPEARE
Measure for Measure, act 1, scene 2, 1604

The calla lilies are in bloom again.
Such a strange flower, suitable to any occasion.
I carried them on my wedding day
and now I place them here
in memory of something that has died.

—KATHARINE HEPBURN
  as Terry Randall, *Stage Door*, 1937

These lines are among the most famous Katharine Hepburn ever uttered, first in the Broadway play *The Lake* (1933) and again in 1937, when she starred in the film *Stage Door*. While the play was a critical flop and one of her biggest failures, the film was a box-office success, whereupon the lines became one of her signature catchphrases.

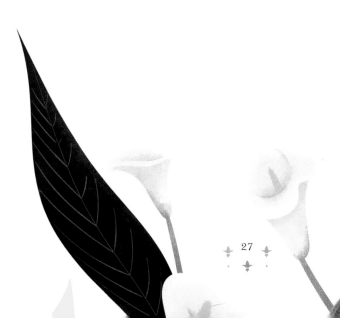

CAMELLIA

Camellia Japonica

RED: My heart bleeds for you
WHITE: Flawless beauty

• ◇ • ◇ • ◇ • ◇ •

ometimes called the Japan rose, *Camellia japonica* was cultivated in China and Japan for many centuries before arriving in Europe in the eighteenth century. Although there are many varieties of camellia, *camellia japonica* has remained the most popular and enduring due to its hardiness and beauty. In China and Japan, the flower was commonly used for ornamental gardening, its leaves for tea, and the oil extracted from its seeds for washing or moisturizing the hair and body. The Chinese consider the camellia a symbol of luck for the new year. Along with the sacred lily, they often offer camellias to various gods for prosperity.

The white camellia has also served as a political symbol. In 1893, New Zealand became the first country to give women the right to vote. During the petitions and rallies leading up to the enactment of the bill, suffragettes gave white camellias to their supporters in Parliament to wear in their buttonholes, and the flower became an emblem of the movement. Anti-suffragists wore red camellias.

In the late 1730s, English botanist Robert James Petre, who had acquired a red camellia seed from an unknown source, was recorded as the first person in Europe to cultivate the flower, which he did in his hothouse garden at Thorndon Hall in Essex. Later, in 1792, as the tea trade between Europe and China expanded, two new varieties, the Alba Plena and Variegata, were introduced by Captain John Corner of the ship *East-India Merchantman Carnatic*. At the time, many shipping captains were encouraged to bring plant samples back from their journeys for wealthy horticulturists; in this case Corner brought the plants for the ship's owner, Gilbert Slater. There is no record of what happened to these two cultivars after Slater's death, but it's believed that sometime in the 1820s, they were transported to the gardens at Chiswick House in West London, the residence of William, the 5th Duke of Devonshire. There the duke had built a three-hundred-foot-tall glass greenhouse, which was not only one of the largest camellia conservatories in the world, but also held one of the largest camellia collections of the era.

After the introduction of these two cultivars to Chiswick, the camellia's popularity in the Victorian garden and for use as a delicately flavored tea spread rapidly, even though it was still considered an exotic. Expensive to obtain, it was primarily kept by women whose households could afford to maintain large outdoor gardens. Those who were able to cultivate camellias found them easy to grow and considered them to be even more beautiful than roses. It was also fashionable to wear the flowers in the hair or pinned to a dress, or to bring a bouquet of them to a party.

The camellia has had many admirers, but none that personified its elegance as closely as Coco Chanel. There are many theories about how Chanel came to adore the flower, from reading Alexandre Dumas's novel *La Dame aux Camélias* to seeing Sarah Bernhardt perform in its stage adaptation to receiving a bouquet of the flowers from a suitor (rumored to have been the polo player Arthur "Boy" Capel, in 1912). However she had been introduced to the camellia, it became and has long been a signature of the House of Chanel, a motif that has been incorporated

into its full range of couture, ready-to-wear clothing, and accessories. Interestingly, one of the qualities Chanel herself loved most about the flower was that it bore no scent and could therefore be worn on her jacket without interfering with her personal fragrance, Chanel No. 5.

PROUST'S CAMELLIA

I felt when I looked at Rosemonde—flooded with a sulphurous rose colour, with the further contrast of the greenish light in her eyes— and then at Andrée—whose white cheeks received such an austere distinction from her black hair—the same kind of pleasure as if I had been looking alternately at a geranium growing by a sunlit sea and a camellia in the night.

—MARCEL PROUST
  Within a Budding Grove, Volume 2, 1923

Between 1890 and 1920, Marcel Proust often wore a camellia pinned to his lapel, supposedly as a sign of refinement. His former housekeeper, Céleste Albaret, wrote a biography, *Monsieur Proust*, in which she recounted that he himself referred to this era as his "camellia buttonhole" period. In William C. Carter's biography, *Marcel Proust: A Life*, it's noted that Proust often wore a camellia, which was "the flower in vogue among the smart set." Members of Proust's social circle at that time were varied and included other writers such as Robert de Flers, Lucien Daudet (son of the novelist Alphonse Daudet), Fernand Gregh, the French historian Daniel Halévy, French doctor Jacques Bizet, and many more. Camellias are also frequently mentioned in Proust's classic novel, *In Search of Lost Time*.

CARNATION

Dianthus caryophyllus

RED: Pure love
WHITE: Talent
YELLOW: Disdain

· ◇ · ◇ ·◇· ◇ ·

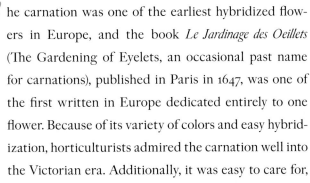

he carnation was one of the earliest hybridized flowers in Europe, and the book *Le Jardinage des Oeillets* (The Gardening of Eyelets, an occasional past name for carnations), published in Paris in 1647, was one of the first written in Europe dedicated entirely to one flower. Because of its variety of colors and easy hybridization, horticulturists admired the carnation well into the Victorian era. Additionally, it was easy to care for, highly ornamental, and, as early American gardening writer Louise Beebe Wilder describes, a "gay and fragrant flower."

In Henry Phillips's *Floral Emblems*, he writes that the red carnation is simply a fragrant beauty that's deserving of its ranking and symbolism in the language of flowers. Of the white carnation he says that the flower is so "richly gifted with odour" that this makes it emblematic of "those persons who benefit society by their talents," an interesting observation in light of the custom at the University of Oxford for students to wear a carnation during exams: white for the first, pink for the intermediates, and red for the last. Regarding the yellow carnation, however, Phillips notes that this color is more acceptable to a florist than to a lover. He writes that this is because yellow is an unfortunate reminder of Selim I, sultan of the Ottoman Empire, who had a tendency to cut off the heads of any Greeks he saw wearing yellow boots.

Carnations are a flowering herbaceous plant of the *Dianthus* genus, which also includes the pink and sweet William species. The name *Dianthus* comes from the Greek words *dios* and *anthos*, meaning "divine flower" and was first given in the book *Enquiry into Plants*, written by the Greek botanist Theophrastus some-time between 350 and 287 BC. Exact origins of the species are unclear, but they are largely known to be native to Eurasia. In Henry Lyte's *A niewe Herball*, he generally describes carnations as sweet William and *gillofers*, an Old English name for gillyflowers.

Unlike sweet William, which is a species, *gillyflower* is a descriptive term that generally refers to many types of fragrant flowers. Lyte described the flowers' colors as white, deep red, bright red, speckled, and "carnation." In Old English *carnation* became the name used to refer to a pinkish color of skin. He also wrote that, when combined with sugar, carnations not only comfort the heart but are useful against hot fevers and pestilence.

According to Louise Beebe Wilder's *The Fragrant Path*, the term *gillyflower* may have been a corruption of a French word *giroflée*, which described the spicy clove-like scent of the carnation and its use as a cheaper alternative to Indian clove. The word *carnation* seems to have come about sometime in the 1530s as a corruption of the word *coronation*, as it was often used in flower crowns and garlands, and the jagged edges of the petals make the flowers resemble a crown.

There is a commonly repeated story about the carnation's beginnings, although the story's origins are not clear, either. In Greek mythology, the carnation was created by the goddess of the hunt and the moon, Artemis. (In Roman mythology, Artemis is also known as Diana, which creates a further connection between the myth and the flower's Latin name, *Dianthus*.)

All versions of the story include Artemis, who encounters a handsome youth as she returns home from a deer hunt. In some versions of the myth, Artemis and the youth fall in love, with discord soon to follow, while in others she blames him for a poor hunt. In both stories, the result is the same: Artemis becomes vexed and tears or shoots out his eyes—and carnations grow from the spot where they land on the ground, possibly symbolizing innocent blood spilled or Artemis's regret for her actions.

During the late Victorian era, writer and dandy Oscar Wilde favored wearing green carnations and would have his friends wear them too, to signify that they were all in the same group. Some biographers have speculated that this was symbolic of homosexuality, although Wilde himself never suggested that it was. He seems to have preferred to leave its significance to the imagination of those who questioned it. If anything, an unnaturally green-tinted carnation was emblematic of one of his favorite ideas from the Decadent movement: Nature should, and often does, imitate art. In a letter he wrote to the *Pall Mall Gazette*, denying his authorship of the anonymously published novel *The Green Carnation*, he referred to the flower as "a work of art." Based on the romantic relationship between Oscar Wilde and his friend Lord Alfred Douglas, the book was satirical, yet scandalous enough to be used as evidence against Wilde in two court trials for the crime of gross indecency, for which he ended up being sentenced to two years of hard labor. The novel was later revealed to have been written by the English journalist Robert Hichens.

• ◊ • ◊ • • ◊ • ◊ •

To the Elysian shades dismiss my soul,

where no carnation fades.

—ALEXANDER POPE
  *The works of Alexander Pope. With his last corrections, additions,
  and improvements.* Publ. by mr. Warburton. With occasional notes, 1751

Five hundred
White Carnations

Carnations have a long association with Mother's Day. Mother's Day origi-
nated as Mother's Friendship Day, an annual event initiated in 1868 by Ann
Reeves Jarvis, an American activist and community organizer who focused
largely on the needs of women with children during the American Civil War.
She conceived of the day as a time when mothers of soldiers from both the
North and South could come together and try to foster peace.

On May 10, 1908, three years after Jarvis died, her daughter Anna Marie
Jarvis held a memorial in her honor in two locations: the church where her
mother had taught Sunday school in Grafton, Virginia, and in Philadelphia,
where Anna was living at the time. Anna attended the Philadelphia ceremony and gave a speech in defense of adopting Mother's Day as a national
holiday. In place of attending the Grafton ceremony, she sent five hundred
white carnations, her mother's favorite flower, to be distributed among the
guests and children. She later explained that a white carnation also stands for
the purity, truth, and charity of a mother's love, and that even the tenacious
way that carnations hug their petals as they die is similar to the way that
mothers hold their children close. The memorial marked the first Mother's
Day, and since then, carnations have represented the holiday.

CHERRY BLOSSOM

Prunus serrulata

Spiritual beauty

• ◇ • ◇ • ◇ • ◇ •

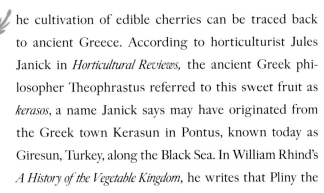he cultivation of edible cherries can be traced back to ancient Greece. According to horticulturist Jules Janick in *Horticultural Reviews,* the ancient Greek philosopher Theophrastus referred to this sweet fruit as *kerasos*, a name Janick says may have originated from the Greek town Kerasun in Pontus, known today as Giresun, Turkey, along the Black Sea. In William Rhind's *A History of the Vegetable Kingdom*, he writes that Pliny the Elder had recorded that Lucullus, a Roman general and politician who had conquered the ancient city of Mithridates in Pontus, had been the first person to bring edible cherries to Europe around 67–68 BC. According to Janick, though, these cherries had already been cultivated in Italy and other parts of Europe well before Lucullus, so, while many botanists speculate that they are not native to Europe, there's no clear answer as to how they arrived there. We do know that when cherries reached England, Henry VIII certainly enjoyed them. According to notes made in the memoranda of the English antiquary and writer John Aubrey in the late 1600s, cherries were imported by the king, "who being in Flanders, and likeing ye Cherries, ordered his Gardiner, brought ym thence, and propagated them in England, particularly in Kent, which soile is most proper for them."

Cherry trees are of the *Prunus* genus in the Rosaceae family, which also includes almonds, peaches, plums, and apricots. The exact origin of the cherry tree is unknown, although many varieties can be traced to North America, Europe, and Asia, and there are fossil records from as early as the Bronze Age. The species from which we harvest edible cherries are believed to be native to western Asia and eastern Europe; the species that is part of the vocabulary of the Victorian language of flowers, *Prunus serrulata*, is native to Japan, China, and Korea. This species is more commonly known as the Japanese flowering cherry. In Japan it is called *sakura*, a word that has also become the general term for cherry blossom.

The Victorians were fond of edible cherries and their lightly scented blossoms, and they often cultivated them as an ornamental and snack-bearing addition to the garden. An annual magazine, *The Gardeners' Chronicle* noted in its 1841 issue that the cherry *Prunus avium*, which we know today as the Royal Ann cherry, was highlighted as "a sort well deserving of cultivation" because of how abundantly the fruit grew on the tree compared to other varieties and how large and dark the cherries were. Wild cherry trees were also often planted in order to help protect other trees and plants growing around them from the wind and sun. The journal advised planting cherry trees in light soil and using them as a nurse or subsidiary to other larger trees such as the oak, ash, or elm because the cherry tree grows quickly, does not overshadow other plants, and is flexible enough to give way to these other trees as they mature. Older cherry trees were recommended as being a good source of timber for fence posts and railings.

In 1853, Japan ended its isolationist foreign policy, which had cut the country off from the rest of the world for more than two hundred years. As imports began to pour in from Japan, a fascination with the exoticism of Japanese art and culture took such a hold on Western societies that the French coined the term *Japonisme*. Although this term was often used to describe the broad influence of Japanese culture on Europeans, it more specifically referred to its influence on European art of the time, particularly impressionism. Victorians began to incorporate kimono-style shapes and fabric into their clothing; Japanese motifs of birds and flowers (especially cherry blossoms) began to appear in Victorian artworks; Japanese fans became a popular accessory; and a Victorian parlor wasn't complete without a Japanese-style tea set.

In art, woodblock prints from the Edo period in the style known as *ukiyo-e*, or "floating world," experienced a resurgence in France and England. As Colta Feller Ives writes in her book *The Great Wave: The Influence of Japanese Woodcuts on French Prints*, these works would often feature motifs that referenced floating such as "the pleasures of the moon, the snow, the cherry blossoms, and the maple leaves." Vincent van Gogh, Claude Monet, Paul Gauguin, and even the French composer Claude Debussy were just a few of the prominent artists who had found themselves quickly swept up in this movement. Upon returning home to England from a trip he took to Japan in 1887, the Australian artist Mortimer Menpes, a pupil of James McNeill Whistler, chose to adopt the Japanese tradition of decorating each room in his house with one beautiful flower. In Ayako Ono's *Japonisme in Britain: Whistler, Menpes, Henry, Hornel and Nineteenth-century Japan*, she writes that he chose to do this by carving the flowers into pieces of wood he had selected in Osaka, and that it took two years for English workmen to finish installing them in the house. Menpes selected a camellia for his studio, a peony for his drawing room, chrysanthemums for his halls, and a cherry blossom for his dining room.

• ◊ • ◊ • ◊ • ◊ •

If earth but ceas'd to offer to my sight
The beauteous cherry-trees when blossoming,
Ah! Then indeed, with peaceful, pure delight,
My heart might revel in the joys of spring!

—ARIWARA NO NARIHIRA
Kokinshū, Book I, Spring I, 55 (905), *The Classical Poetry of the Japanese*, 1880

HELLO, HANAMI

In Japan, the cherry blossom holds significant cultural importance and symbolism. The time of honoring their annual blooming period is a nationally observed celebration, referred to as *hanami*. The first recording of *hanami* is written in *The Nihon Shoki* (*The Chronicles of Japan*), which can be traced back to the third century AD. Although *hanami* translates to "flower viewing" and has included Chinese plum blossoms in the past, over the centuries the term has become synonymous with *sakura* and today refers to cherry blossoms.

Nonetheless, the blooming of the cherry blossom is such an important annual event that the Japanese Meteorological Agency tracks the opening of the blossoms as the season begins, originating in the south and moving north. The Japanese pay close attention to these reports so that they can plan for ritual viewing parties and picnics with friends and family. Because of how quickly the flowers bloom and fade, the Japanese believe they symbolize the beautiful but fleeting nature of life.

CHRYSANTHEMUM

Chrysanthemum indicum

Cheerfulness under adversity

• ◇ • ◇ • ◇ • ◇ • ◇ •

ith records of their cultivation and use in herbal teas and medicines dating from as early as 1500 BC, chrysanthemums come primarily from China. The name *chrysanthemum* comes from the Ancient Greek words *chryssos* (meaning "gold") and *anthemom* (meaning "flower"). The flowers are sometimes called mums and belong to the extensive Asteraceae family, which also includes daisies, sunflowers, dahlias, dandelions, artichokes, lettuce, and many other species.

In the Victorian garden, chrysanthemums were regarded as a hardy perennial flower with a happy appearance and a scent similar to chamomile. Some species have also been described as having a bitter or spicy scent, which Louise Beebe Wilder refers to as a "nose-twister"—similar to the scent of nasturtiums—in her book *The Fragrant Path*. Popular for their large, button- or globe-shaped blooms and variety of colors, chrysanthemums were frequently showcased in flower shows and conferences all over Victorian England. An entry from *The Gardeners' Chronicle* for 1841 explains that the novelty of chrysanthemums gave such "sport into endless variations of form, size, and colour," which led to its classification as a Florist's Flower, a special distinction made by floral societies for a small group of highly variable

species. As a Florist's Flower, new varieties of chrysanthemums were judged by a strict set of rules to determine their quality.

In Henry Phillips's *Floral Emblems*, he describes the chrysanthemum as a flower that gives "so much cheerfulness," even under winter weather conditions, which makes it the perfect symbol for an "enviable disposition" and of cheerfulness under adversity. Elizabeth Washington Wirt's *Flora's Dictionary* and Kate Greenaway's *Language of Flowers* give additional meanings to different colors: to rose, "I love"; to white, "truth"; and to yellow, "slighted love." Unfortunately, explanations for these meanings aren't provided, but it's possible to draw inferences from the Victorian attitude toward these colors in descriptions of other, similar-colored flowers. Red or pink colors typically stand in for positive feelings of love. White usually represents truth or purity and yellow is usually only ever admired by florists, such as with yellow carnations. In Beverly Seaton's *The Language of Flowers*, she explains that chrysanthemums were considered a symbol of autumn and merriment by Victorians but that in China they were known as the flower of the "ninth month" or moon, and a symbol of endurance.

The Chongyang Festival (meaning "The Double Ninth" Festival, held on the ninth day of the ninth lunar month of the year), also known as The Chrysanthemum Festival, is a centuries-old Chinese holiday that's also observed in Taiwan, Korea, and Japan. It began in China during the Han dynasty sometime between 206 BC and AD 220 and it represents cleansing the house and body of negative energy and spirits. On this day, it is customary to eat nine-layer steamed rice and nut-and-red-date confections known as *Chongyang* cakes, and to drink chrysanthemum wine. Climbing a mountain is a traditional activity, too. In China and Taiwan, it is also observed as a day to honor senior citizens.

CHRYSANTHEMUM NOTES

Chrysanthemums were commonly found in the gardens of ancient Egypt. The Egyptians would sometimes use the flowers in religious ceremonies and in decorative bouquets. Remnants of chrysanthemums have been found in burial tombs as parts of floral burial collars, and the flowers were also occasionally used as a model for "Egyptian rosettes," which are decorative elements often found in ancient Egyptian décor and used as inlays on a variety of surfaces from ceilings in tombs and temples to the surfaces of objects such as chests and boats.

• ◇ •

In a study done by NASA in 1989, chrysanthemums were shown to be one of a few houseplants that help reduce air pollution and improve indoor air quality.

• ◇ •

Photojournalist Marc Riboud's iconic photograph, *The Ultimate Confrontation: The Flower and the Bayonet*, taken in 1967, depicts seventeen-year-old American Jan Rose Kasmir during a Vietnam War protest. In it, she stands holding a single chrysanthemum before a line of bayonet-wielding soldiers. The image juxtaposes the innocence of an unarmed teenager with outfitted military men and was one of many powerful images that helped further strengthen the "Flower Power" protest slogan during the era.

• ◇ • ◇ • ◇• ◇ •

She is tolerable, but not handsome enough to tempt me,
and I am in no humor at present to give consequence to
young ladies who are slighted by other men.

—MR. DARCY
in *Pride and Prejudice* by Jane Austen, 1813

DAFFODIL

Narcissus

Self-love

• ◇ • ◇ • ◇ • ◇ •

he daffodil, also commonly known by its genus name *Narcissus*, is an ancient flower native to southern Europe and northern Africa. A member of the Amaryllidaceae family, along with onions and chives, it was first described in Theophrastus's *Enquiry into Plants*, sometime between 350 and 287 BC. In *A niewe Herball*, Henry Lyte suggests from personal experience that, added to boiled water or wine, fresh daffodil root with anise or fennel seed and "a little ginger" is an efficacious treatment against "tough and clammy" congestion.

Victorians enjoyed cultivating the daffodil for its sweet fragrance and ornamentation. As Elizabeth Washington Wirt wrote in *Flora's Dictionary*, daffodils have "the most magnificent flowers, bearing its fine golden chalice, amidst petals of the same color, on a stalk two feet high." In his 1906 guide *The Book of Cut Flowers*, professional flower judge R. P. Brotherston wrote not only that daffodils were an appropriate choice for decorating bridal chambers, but also that long-stem flowers such as daffodils were the most valuable in flower arrangements. He explained that "stem value is strongly marked" in flowers such as tulips and daffodils because their long stems help to emphasize the lightness and natural grace of the blossom. Today, daffodils are given in a bunch as a gift for a variety of occasions such as Easter, birthdays, or to cheer up someone who might be injured or feeling down.

According to Beverly Seaton's *Language of Flowers*, flowers with no scent typically symbolized negative aspects of the personality, whereas fragrant flowers would usually symbolize a moral quality, either good or bad. She also describes how metamorphic myths were commonly woven into flower symbolism. The narcissus is therefore a classic example of a flower that represents both a mythical story (an egotistical youth being turned into a flower) as well as egotism itself.

The name *narcissus* is connected to both the ancient Greek word *narkissos*, meaning *narcotic*, and to the tragic Greek myth of Echo and Narcissus. Echo was a mountain nymph who became enamored with the handsome youth Narcissus, son of the river god Cephissus. Narcissus did not return her love, so she pined away for him until, at last, nothing remained of her except her voice, which would repeat any sounds made in the mountains or valleys. Aphrodite, the goddess of love, punished Narcissus for Echo's demise by causing him to fall in love with his own reflection. Consumed with unrequited love for himself, he refused to leave the reflective pool that was his mirror and wasted away, gradually transforming into a flower.

In a later Greek myth, Persephone, the future wife of Hades, god of the underworld, was lured to abduction by a beautiful yellow narcissus growing by itself in a field. Wandering away from her companions and unable to look away from the striking flower, she was caught off guard as Hades sprang forth from a crevasse and pulled her down into the underworld. At first, Persephone was very unhappy, but she came to love Hades—and the narcissus became a prized flower for them both and is said to grow along the banks of the river Styx in the underworld.

DAFFODIL NOTES

Beware: The daffodil is a toxic plant if eaten uncooked. Many cases of accidental poisoning have been reported for people who mistook the bulb for a leek or an onion.

• ◊ •

Despite its toxic qualities, the narcissus bulb was noted by the Greeks and Romans for use in medicinal treatments of tumors as early as the fourth century BC. The Greek father of medicine, Hippocrates of Kos (c. 460–377 BC), for example, recommended using narcissus oil as a topical treatment for anti-cancer therapy.

• ◊ •

The daffodil was imported to China during the Tang dynasty between AD 618–907, a golden age for artistic and cultural development. The plant was not only incorporated into Chinese landscape gardening but also depicted in paintings and writings, and used medicinally. Another tradition that developed was the art of narcissus bulb carving, a specialized practice of slicing a narcissus bulb so that it grows into specific shapes such as a teapot, crane, rooster, flower vase, or whatever else the carver can imagine. Because the daffodil blooms early in the year, it has also been adopted as a symbol of wealth and good fortune for the Chinese New Year.

• ◊ • ◊ • ◊• ◊ •

I wonder what spendthrift chose to spill
Such a bright gold under my windowsill!
Is it fair gold? Does it glitter still?
Bless me! It's a daffodil!

—CELIA THAXTER
"March," *Stories and Poems for Children,* 1895

Dahlia

Dahlia

Forever thine

• ◇ • ◇ • ◇ • ◇ •

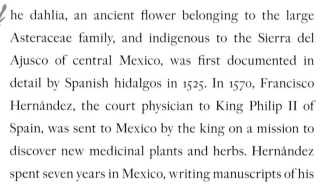

The dahlia, an ancient flower belonging to the large Asteraceae family, and indigenous to the Sierra del Ajusco of central Mexico, was first documented in detail by Spanish hidalgos in 1525. In 1570, Francisco Hernández, the court physician to King Philip II of Spain, was sent to Mexico by the king on a mission to discover new medicinal plants and herbs. Hernández spent seven years in Mexico, writing manuscripts of his discoveries. These recordings included the first written description of dahlias, which were later published in the natural history book *Nova plantarum, animalium et mineralium Mexicanorum historiam* in 1651.

In his book, Hernández wrote that the root of this flower smelled bad and tasted bitter, but that "one ounce eaten relieves stomach ache, helps windiness of the stomach, provokes urine, brings out sweat, drives out chill, strengthens a weak stomach against chill, resists the cholic, opens obstructions, reduces tumors." In addition to medicinal applications, it was recorded that the Aztecs would use the hollow stem of the dahlia for water irrigation and that the Oaxacan people grew the flower as a food crop. Dahlia tubers are similar to potatoes and are still eaten in Oaxacan cuisine today.

In 1787 the French botanist Nicolas-Joseph Thiéry de Menonville was sent to Oaxaca by the French government in search of the cochineal insect, which

can be used for red fabric dye. He reported seeing the plant that Hernández had described growing in this region. Two years later, in 1789, Vicente Cervantes, director of the Botanical Garden at Mexico City, sent a shipment of plant parts to Antonio Jose Cavanilles, the director of the Royal Gardens of Madrid. Cavanilles was able to successfully plant one of the parts from the shipment and, that same year, the first dahlia flower bloomed in Europe. He chose to name it after the Swedish botanist Anders Dahl, a student of Carl Linnaeus, "the father of modern taxonomy." Afterward, Cavanilles sent dahlia seeds to growing houses in Germany, Italy, and France, but their success was limited.

In 1803, the English botanist John Fraser obtained dahlia seeds from Paris and successfully brought them to bloom in his greenhouse at the Apothecaries Garden in London. In 1804, Lady Elizabeth Vassall Fox obtained seeds from Cavanilles and had them sent to her home in Kensington, England. There, her gardener successfully raised the seeds to flower, and in 1806 the distribution of dahlia seeds spread to her friends and other gardeners. It wasn't until 1814 that dahlias became a commonly cultivated flower in the Victorian garden.

Coincidentally, 1804 was also the year that Napoleon Bonaparte became Emperor of France. When the dahlia was introduced to Europe, at the onset of the French Revolution, gardening in France had taken a backseat to political concerns. In the first year of Napoleon's reign, the pastime reemerged, as did the flower, which is why Henry Phillips chose dahlias as a symbol of "instability" in *Floral Emblems.*

Dahlias themselves were also considered to be fickle in the nineteenth century. Early accounts of growing dahlias in England, such as in *The Gardeners' Chronicle* of 1841, note their beauty and elegance and describe how difficult they were to grow. However later, in *The Gardeners' Chronicle* of 1906, the flowers were described as beautiful, easy to propagate, hardy, and mold resistant. *The dahlia; its culture, uses and history,* written in 1847 by the British gardening writer George William Johnson, describes dahlias as "the most beautiful of our autumn flowers." In *Flora's Dictionary*, dahlias are described as a flower with "large and handsome" blossoms, "something like those of a sunflower, but the rays mostly red, or purple, like the China-Aster." It's also noted that, through cultivation, the flowers of the dahlia and the China aster have been doubled and quadrupled, with a significant increase in available sizes and color varieties. Unfortunately, while there is plenty of evidence indicating that the dahlia was enjoyed by Victorian gardeners, there isn't much discussion about its use in arrangements. In modern bridal bouquets, dahlias are viewed as a more elegant alternative to roses or peonies.

· ◇ · ◇ · ◇ · ◇ ·

In Pleasure's dream or Sorrow's hour,
In crowded hall or lonely bower,
The business of my life shall be,
For ever to remember thee.

—THOMAS MOORE
"To ...., 1801,"
The Poetical Works of Thomas Moore, 1827

IMPRESSIONIST DAHLIAS

The French impressionist painter Claude Monet had a strong appreciation for gardening as well as painting, with many of his works being inspired by and completed within his own privately created botanical oasis. His house and gardens, which can still be visited today in Giverny, France, contain his famous water lilies as well as a large variety of other flowers, including dahlias. Varieties that can still be spotted around the garden include the Bishop of Llandaff scarlet dahlia, a single variety of the flower, and a decorative orange dinner plate (meaning flowers measuring eight inches or more in diameter), which grows up to twelve feet high. According to Derek Fell's *The Secrets of Monet's Garden*, Monet had a preference for single over double flowers, possibly because of the translucent petals, which allow light to pass through from behind while also reflecting light that hits the front.

Monet's close friend and fellow painter Pierre-Auguste Renoir was also heavily influenced by gardens. In 1875, he had rented a temporary studio in the district of Montmartre in Paris so that he could be near to the Moulin de la Galette, a subject he'd been wanting to paint and that later became one of his more well-known works. The studio came with an overgrown garden that happened to contain dahlias. Often, the flowers would find their way into Renoir's more decorative compositions, such as *Garden in the Rue Cortot, Montmartre*, a large landscape-size painting depicting two men talking in an overgrown garden filled with dahlias. In a calculated effort to show that decorative subjects could hold the same value for commissions as portraits or scenes of modern life, he brought the painting to the 1877 *L'Impressioniste* exhibition. The work was well received and praised by his friend, art critic and writer Georges Rivière, for its "magnificent red dahlias amidst a jumble of grass and creepers."

DAISY

Bellis perennis

WHITE: Innocence

• ◇ • ◇ • ◇ • ◇ •

A native of Europe, the daisy grows easily and abundantly as a wildflower in meadows and on roadsides, but it has also maintained popularity as an ornamental garden and bouquet flower throughout the centuries. Its genus, *Bellis*, is derived from the Latin *bellus*, meaning "pretty" or "handsome," although an alternative interpretation attributes the roots of the plant's name to the Latin *bello*, meaning "war." Its common name, *daisy*, comes from the Old English *dægeseag*, which means "day's eye." This last meaning originated from the daisy's unique routine of being open during the day, like a golden eye rousing itself for the sun, then closing up to sleep for the night. Daisies are flowering herbaceous plants in the Asteraceae family with white petals that can occasionally have red-tipped edges. There are many species of daisy in a variety of colors, but it is the *Bellis perennis*, the English daisy, that is considered to be the true daisy. It is certainly the variety that is the most written about in lore and poetry.

According to T. F. Dyer's *The Folklore of Plants*, throughout the ages, the daisy has represented superstitious meanings regarding love. He writes that "rustic" European maidens would put daisy roots under their pillows to induce dreams of their would-be suitors. He also describes an old game that is still known today: By plucking the petals off a daisy, one by one, alternating

DELICATE & LASTING PLEASURES
ARISING FROM THE CUP OF INNOCENCE

Daisy cup with sweet peas inspired by an illustration from
Henry Phillips's *Floral Emblems* (1825)

the phrases *loves me* and *loves me not*, lovestruck youths can predict whether an object of affection returns their feelings. The phrase that falls on the last remaining petal reveals the answer. Daisies' long stems can be threaded into garlands or daisy chains, and made into crowns or bracelets. In Lewis Carroll's *Alice's Adventures in Wonderland*, Alice contemplates "the pleasure of making a daisy-chain" to keep herself busy. In *Floral Emblems*, Henry Phillips notes that the daisy was "one of the earliest floral amusements of infancy" and has therefore come to symbolize innocence.

Flora's Dictionary notes that the daisy's significance is defined by passages from famous authors that describe its romantic and admirable beauty. Most notably, in Percy Bysshe Shelley's poem "The Question," he compares the daisy to the star Arcturus, the brightest star of the constellation Boötes and the brightest star of the northern celestial hemisphere. He writes: "*Daisies*, those pearled Arcturi of the earth,/The constellated flower that never sets . . ." And Elizabeth Washington Wirt writes that daisies not only cast a "lustre over rural scenery" with their "constellated beauty" but that, like the star Arcturus, their bloom is ever present and can be singled out as the "most admirable" in the surrounding collection of natural beautiful things.

* ◇ * ◇ * ◇ * ◇ *

I see thee glittering from afar; —
And then thou art a pretty Star;
Not quite so fair as many are
In heaven above thee!
Yet like a star, with glittering crest,
Self-poised in air though seem'st to rest; —
May peace come never to his nest,
Who shall reprove thee!

—WILLIAM WORDSWORTH
"To the Daisy," *The Complete Poetical Works of William Wordsworth*, 1837

As Refreshing as a Daisy

Eighteenth- and early-nineteenth-century etiquette manuals often suggested throwing a daisy-themed tea party. Here's an excerpt from Clara Laughlin's 1906 *The Complete Hostess*: "For a daisy tea have the room decorated with ferns and daisies. If possible, have the napkins of the color of the flower scheme. Let the butter be in daisy form. The white *menu* cards should have a daisy painted on the outside and should have a bow of yellow ribbon. The *menu* may be chicken salad, rolls, olives, orange cake, and ices."

Effie Merriman's 1891 book, *Socials*, which provides instructions for planning and executing themed fund-raising parties, offers a "conundrum social." In the described event, two boxes are set near the entrance of the party room. One is full of "conundrums" written on strips of paper, while the other box contains strips of paper with the answers on them. Whenever a gentleman enters the room, he must select a strip from the answer box; when a lady enters, she must select a conundrum.

During the party, the men must begin conversations with the women in order to find the one whose conundrum he believes matches his answer. To check if he's correct, he must escort her to the manager of the event, who has the full list of matches. If the man is correct, he buys the woman's dinner; if he's incorrect, he must pay a fine of five cents, which goes toward the cause at hand.

Anyone at the event who remains unmatched is a "daisy." The daisies are: "consoled for their sad fate by having special favors heaped upon them. A "daisy tea" (The daisy is an entirely edible plant. The young leaves and flower heads can be eaten raw as well as steeped for tea) is provided for them at a special table decorated with daisies and spread with dainties that the other tables do not have. They each wear a daisy, and after supper have the privilege of selecting whom they wish among the crowd for a partner in the first game, or for a special tête-à-tête if games are not played, and the rightful partner can offer no objections." Merriman also suggests that "this social may be varied in a community of readers, by writing a well-known quotation on a card instead of a conundrum."

FORGET·ME·NOT

Myosotis

True love

• ◇ • ◇ • ◇ • ◇ •

The forget-me-not has been known as a symbol of love and remembrance since the medieval ages in both historical and mythological contexts. In 1398 Henry of Lancaster, later King Henry IV, was banished from England by his cousin, King Richard II, possibly as a form of revenge for joining opposition leaders that had outlawed Richard's closest associates and advisers a year earlier. Publicly however, Richard claimed that the banishment was to prevent Henry from participating in a duel with Thomas de Mowbray, the 1st Duke of Norfolk.

While Henry was in exile, he chose the forget-me-not as his personal emblem because he wanted his people to remember him. The following year, he returned to the kingdom and overthrew Richard. Once Henry became king, he made the flower his official symbol.

English historian Charles Mills shares a frequently repeated German medieval legend about a knight who was in love with a lady. Mills doesn't give a title for this tale, but most sources refer to it as some variation of "The Legend of the Forget-me-Not"; the original author is unknown. As the story goes, the two lovers were taking a walk by the edge of a lake one evening when the maiden spotted clusters of little blue flowers growing on the opposite bank. She wished to possess these flowers, so her knight dove into the water while wearing his full suit of armor to fetch them for her. With the flowers in hand, he began swimming back to her, but the weight of his armor was quickly draining his energy and he began to sink. As he drowned, he threw the bouquet toward the maiden while shouting for her to never forget him.

In a retelling of this story from Laura Valentine's Victorian book *Beautiful Bouquets Culled from the Poets of All Countries*, Albert, a knight, and Ida, a lady, are outside on a walk together. Ida sees the flowers on an island in the middle of a lake, and as Albert swims to gather them for her, he encounters "rising waves, which foamed in wrath, as if some spirit's hand awoke the genii of the lake to guard their mystic land." While trying in vain to swim back to Ida, the water's "angry waves" pull him to his death. As he sinks, the flowers fall to her feet and he exclaims, "Ida, forget me not!"

Valentine includes another poem, "The Bride of the Danube," which tells the same story, but in this case, it is the male who spots the flowers. He wishes to bring them to his fiancée so that they can "form a braid for thy sunny hair." His lady begs him to stay with her, but it is too late, for he has already jumped into the water and been swept away to his death by a flood.

While forget-me-nots have inspired many old tales, they were often employed as a decorative motif to embellish medieval manuscripts or incorporated into paintings with love-related themes. One such example is a double-sided portrait by German painter Hans Süss von Kulmbach. One side of the 1508 work depicts *Portrait of a Young Man*, which contains a close-up portrait of a young man. The other side contains *Girl Making a Garland*, which depicts a maiden making a garland out of forget-me-nots with a decorative banner floating above her head that reads, "I bind with forget-me-nots" in German. According to the Metropolitan Museum of Art, which owns the painting, these portraits appear to symbolize a young bride-to-be "promising to bind her heart faithfully" to the young man. The painting also prominently features a cat, which has been interpreted as another symbol of devotion used in art throughout the ages.

In *The Gardeners' Chronicle* of 1895, forget-me-nots were described as an old-fashioned yet "universal favorite" in the Victorian garden and "amongst

our most beautiful spring flowering plants." They are also easy to cultivate, accessible, and work well as an accent in smaller bouquets.

Although we primarily know this flower as the forget-me-not, it is also sometimes called scorpion grass because of its stems' tendency to grow in a curved shape resembling a scorpion's tail. Meanwhile its scientific name, *Myosotis*, is a Latin variation of the ancient Greek word *muosōtis*, meaning "mouse's ears," for the resemblance of its foliage to the animal's ears. In Henry Lyte's *A niewe Herball*, he writes that scorpion grass was useful to help with the stinging caused by a scorpion, which the Greek botanist and physician Pedanius Dioscorides had previously suggested in *De Materia Medica*, written between AD 50 and 70. In contrast to this, according to the writings of Hildegard von Bingen, a nun and medieval healer who lived almost four hundred years before Lyte wrote his book, the forget-me-not is useless as a medicine and would cause more harm than good if ingested. In view of Lyte's and Dioscorides's ancient medical advice, this author has labored and must confess she has not yet encountered any references to using this flower for the treatment of a mouse bite.

Today, these little blue flowers continue to be enjoyed in gardens and bouquets for their quaint charm. Not only are they still used as a motif in jewelry and home décor, but they are also commonly incorporated into tattoo designs. In modern wedding bouquets they are often used as "something blue" to be borne by the bride.

• ◊ • ◊ • ◊ • ◊ •

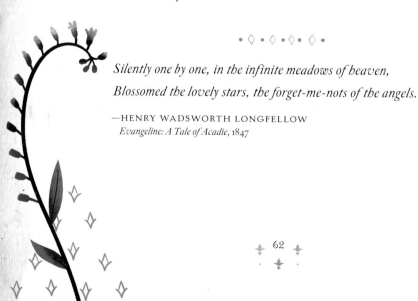

Silently one by one, in the infinite meadows of heaven,
Blossomed the lovely stars, the forget-me-nots of the angels.

—HENRY WADSWORTH LONGFELLOW
Evangeline: A Tale of Acadie, 1847

WIDOWS' WEEDS

While Victorians incorporated forget-me-nots into porcelain tea sets, Valentine's Day cards, and keepsake boxes, they also used the flowers in jewelry such as rings, bracelets, and brooches that were often worn as part of a mourning ensemble.

The customs surrounding mourning the loss of a loved one were taken very seriously by Victorians and were expected to be observed by women, children, and even babies, whose crib blankets would sometimes be embroidered with black thread. Men were only required to wear a black sash or armband. A widow was expected to observe three terms of mourning: the first, lasting for one year and one day; the second, for nine months; and the third, for six months. She was not permitted to engage in any social activities or outings for at least the first six months. This period was followed by another six months of socializing with only close relatives. She could not attend any balls or parties until the complete mourning period was finished. In the first two terms, she would wear dull black clothing made of silk and crepe with a collar and sleeves trimmed in white. In the final stage, she would wear the muted half-mourning colors of gray, purple, or white—tones less somber than black, but still not joyful. The duration of mourning would change depending on a person's relationship to the deceased. The mourning period observed after the death of a husband was the longest. The period following the death of a child, sibling, or parent was half as long, while the expected time for mourning an in-law, aunt, uncle, or cousin might only last about one month.

To complete the mourning look, the correct accessories were required. A black or purple handkerchief was a must, while jet and black enamel rings, bracelets, and necklaces bearing inscriptions were popular. Sometimes these items would even include a lock of the deceased's hair that had been glazed into the enamel. Accessories made from hair were even fashionable to wear when people were not in mourning and could be given as tokens of friendship or admiration.

FOXGLOVE

Digitalis purpurea

Wishfulness

• ◇ • ◇ • ◇ • ◇ •

oxglove's genus, *Digitalis*, was given by the botanist Leonard Fuchs in 1542 as a New Latin translation of the German word *fingerhut*, which literally translates as "thimble." In *Flora's Dictionary*, Elizabeth Washington Wirt writes that *digitalis* is derived from *digitale,* meaning "finger of a glove," however *digitales* is the singular Latin for "of or belonging to a finger," with nary a mention of a glove. The foxglove is a flowering plant of the Plantaginaceae (or plantain) family that's primarily native to western, southern, and central Europe and produces tall spires of long, bell-shaped flowers that can easily fit over one's fingertip. A few alternate names for this flower include *folks' glove, witches' bells,* or *witches' thimble,* all of which reference Nordic and European lore. In these stories, fairies would use the flowers as thimbles to mend their clothes or witches would decorate their fingers with the blooms.

As for the flower's relationship to foxes, etymologist Anatoly Liberman believes that the *fox* may have originally been *folks* and that, over time, names such as *folks' glove* were shortened to *foxglove*. Any relation to actual foxes would be entirely mythical. For instance, in his book *Flowers and Flower Lore*, English botanist Hilderic Friend writes that the Norwegian name for this flower, *foxes-gleow*, roughly translates to "fox-music" and that in Welsh lore, foxgloves were thought to be used by fairies as musical bells. Because foxgloves commonly grow in areas that foxes are known to frequent, Friend draws a general connection between the music of the fairies and the music of the foxes—for whatever that's worth.

Although highly toxic if misused, the foxglove has been recorded as an herbal medicine for many centuries, specifically as a treatment for heart and kidney problems. In *A niewe Herball*, Henry Lyte writes that foxglove could be boiled in wine or water and taken to help clear congestion caused by fever or any "stoppings" of the liver, spleen, and other internal organs. According to Friend, in the seventeenth century, Italians frequently applied foxglove topically to cleanse and heal wounds.

In *The Gardeners' Chronicle* of 1874, foxgloves were described as "stately" and well placed in a "wild garden," where plants are free to grow more naturally, the way they might in the woods or along a riverbank. Victorians also seemed to enjoy them as indoor table arrangements. In Volume II of *The Florist and Horticultural Journal*, a journalist describes "one of the prettiest sights" of an 1853 visit to The New York Horticultural Society's semiannual exhibition as a circular table set with a variety of "handsome" bouquets, one of which was a tall pyramid-shaped bouquet in a vase that consisted of "a very pretty variety of the common *digitalis* or foxglove." Today foxgloves continue to be enjoyed for their elegant yet whimsical appearance and work well in spring-themed bouquets.

• ◊ • ◊ •◊• ◊ •

Would that I were
A sound that I might steal upon thy dreams,
And, like the breathing of my flute, distil
Sweetly upon thy senses.

—NATHANIEL PARKER WILLIS
  "The Serenade," *Fugitive Poetry*, 1829

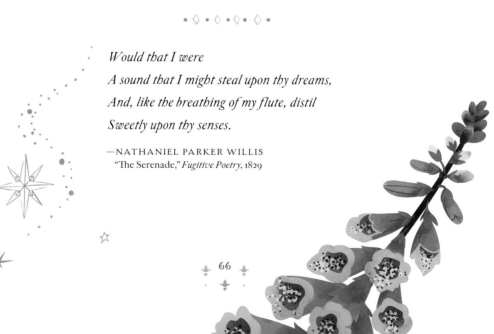

SEEING YELLOW

Although he was never formally diagnosed with epilepsy, it is possible Vincent van Gogh may have suffered from the disease in the later years of his life, according to the Van Gogh Museum, which refers to observations by Félix Rey, a doctor at the hospital in Arles where Vincent was staying.

According to Paul Wolf, a clinical professor of pathology at the University of California, in his article "Creativity and Chronic Disease: Vincent van Gogh (1853–1890)," *Digitalis* was a common drug for treating epilepsy at this time and, if overprescribed, could lead to the side effects of *Digitalis* intoxication. These would include seeing halos of light, sometimes surrounded by yellow speckles, and yellow-tinted vision. Two of Van Gogh's paintings created during this time can be characterized as reflecting these effects. The first, *The Starry Night*, displays dotted orbs that could indicate an increased presence of halos of light. The second, *The Night Café*, shows a predominance of yellow. Additionally, one of the artist's more highly regarded paintings is a portrait completed in 1890 of one of his last doctors, Paul-Ferdinand Gachet, who poses with a handful of purple foxglove flowers. Because Van Gogh's letters do not indicate whether or not he was treated with *Digitalis*, no one knows for certain whether he suffered from its effects. However, the portrait of his doctor and certain hallmarks evident in his last works support this interesting but highly speculative theory.

FUCHSIA

Fuchsia

Good taste

• ◊ • ◊ • ◊ • ◊ •

The fuchsia was discovered in the Caribbean in 1696 by the French monk and botanist Charles Plumier, for whom the *Plumeria* plant is named. Plumier chose to name the plant in honor of the highly distinguished German physician and botanist Leonhard Fuchs. The plant is a flowering shrub of the evening primrose, or Onagraceae, family and is native to South America and some parts of Central America.

The name for the color fuchsia was inspired by the flower, which typically grows with bright reddish-pink sepals (outer leaves that encase the flower) and petals of either dark purple or white. The company that gave the color this name was a French manufacturer of fabric dye, Renard Frères et Franc. The word *renard* is French for fox; in German, the word for fox is *fuchs*; and fuchsia flowers were extremely popular in French gardens at the time. With the double meaning of fox in both the name of the flower and the name of the dye manufacturer, the name *fuchsine* was chosen for the shade of vivid purple-red. Later, in celebration of the French victory at the Battle of Magenta during the Second Italian War of Independence, the name was changed to the easier to pronounce *magenta*. It is due to the plant's richly colored blossoms and the graceful way in which they hang that Henry Phillips chose to assign them the meaning of "taste" in his book *Floral Emblems*.

According to the British Fuchsia Society, fuchsias weren't introduced to England until 1788 when Captain Firth, the captain of a ship coming back from South America, brought a specimen to Kew Gardens. Fuchsias do well in hanging baskets and high-humidity conditions which, in addition to their highly ornamental appearance, made them popular in the greenhouse and in interior decorating during the Victorian era. In Annie Hassard's *Floral Decorations for the Dwelling House: A Practical Guide to the Home Arrangement of Plants and Flowers*, she writes that a hanging window basket "never looks well unless it is furnished with some drooping plant around the edge" and that in the center there "should be a well-grown plant of Fuchsia Mrs. Marshall." This specific cultivar has white sepals with a bright rosy pink center and was hybridized in 1862, making it one of the older varieties of fuchsia still around today. In Volume II of *The Florist and Horticultural Journal*, the fuchsia is described as a highly admired plant that, when well grown, can hardly be compared to anything else and makes the best, most distinct display on an exhibition table. James Lye, who was head gardener at Clyffe Hall in Market Lavington during the late nineteenth century, was known as a champion fuchsia grower of West England for his ability to cultivate fuchsia plants as large as ten feet high and five feet wide. Fuchsias continue to be popular in gardening today because they are so visually impactful and require very little care.

◦ ◊ ◦ ◦ ◊ ◦ ◊ ◦

Happiness lies in the taste, and not in the things;
and it is from having what we desire that we are happy—
not from having what others think desirable.

—FRANÇOIS DUC DE LA ROCHEFOUCAULD
  Maximes, 1665

Fuchsia Meets Fashion

A strong and eye-catching color, fuchsia has walked the runway countless times over the years, as designers, including Yves Saint Laurent, have long recognized its power. Saint Laurent, known for his modernism (he introduced ready-to-wear in the 1960s with his Rive Gauche line) and love of color, often incorporated rich tones like sapphire, emerald, and fuchsia into his collections. In fact, fuchsia has become a brand signature over the years.

On December 5, 1983, The Metropolitan Museum of Art held a retrospective exhibition in honor of the designer and twenty-five years of his work. One of Saint Laurent's major fabric suppliers, the Zurich silk house Gustav Zumsteg of Abraham, swathed the entire main hall of the museum in fifteen thousand yards of fuchsia and orange silks, a color combination prevalent in many Saint Laurent ensembles. Bernadine Morris of the *New York Times* wrote of the event, "In varying shades of pink, orange and red, the tables looked like a flower garden. The columns in what was once known as the pool room were draped in similar silks held by garlands of gold leaves."

A few years earlier, in 1979, Yves Saint Laurent launched Rouge Pur Lipstick No. 19, a fuchsia with blue undertones inspired by a piece of fuchsia silk—and it's still the company's best-selling lip color. To honor its place in YSL's history, the company issued Le Fuchsia Collection, a limited edition line of fuchsia lipstick, in 2018.

GERANIUM

Geraniaceae

ROSE-SCENTED GERANIUM: You're my preference
WILD CRANESBILL: Envy

• ◇ • ◇ • ◇ • ◇ •

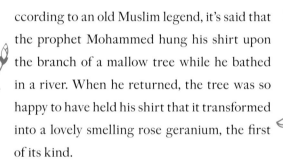

ccording to an old Muslim legend, it's said that the prophet Mohammed hung his shirt upon the branch of a mallow tree while he bathed in a river. When he returned, the tree was so happy to have held his shirt that it transformed into a lovely smelling rose geranium, the first of its kind.

Geraniums are native to the Cape of Good Hope in South Africa and are believed to have been brought to Europe by the Dutch East India Company as a medicine and possible food source sometime between the late sixteenth and early seventeenth centuries. Some historical accounts of the geranium's arrival in Europe indicate that they were first planted in the Leiden Botanical Gardens in the Netherlands but, according to the garden's history, the geranium wasn't brought there until the beginning of the eighteenth century.

One of the earliest European descriptions of geraniums is in *Cruydeboeck* (Dutch for "herb book"), written in 1554 by the Flemish botanist Rembert Dodoens, who frequently references *De Materia Medica*. Nonetheless, it's unclear whether the geranium was in Europe at this time or if the description was simply a reference to the plant, but the book's translation into other languages and various updated editions noted its various uses over the years.

In 1578, the English botanist Henry Lyte translated *Cruydeboeck* from the botanist Carolus Clusius's 1557 French translation, *Histoire des plantes*, and published it as *A niewe Herball, or Historie of plantes*. Lyte's book was the first English edition of *Cruydeboeck* and became the text's standard version. In it, he writes that geraniums were used to treat a variety of illnesses such as ulcers, cuts, skin infections, and kidney stones. In 1597, the botanist John Gerarde published *The herball, or, Generall historie of plantes*, rewriting Lyte's book and supplementing it with new information. Finally, in the third edition of Gerard's book, in 1636, with edits by Thomas Johnson, thus bloomed the geranium, for it was noted that John Tradescant, gardener to King Charles I of England, was the first person to bring geranium seeds to England from South Africa in 1631, achieving the first successful flowering in 1632.

Because they thrived in greenhouses and window boxes, were easy to hybridize, and had many medicinal uses, geraniums were a popular garden plant during the Victorian era. *Flora's Dictionary* notes that the geranium "has not much beauty to recommend it, yet its retiring and modest worth, so generally overlooked in the gay saloon, may well be supposed to excite something like *envy* of its more favored rivals." In other words, what the geranium lacked in beauty it more than made up for in its usefulness. Yet, according to Louise Beebe Wilder's *The Fragrant Path*, the Victorian bouquet was considered incomplete without geraniums. Their notched leaves and small flowers added a lacy decorative element to the outer edge of a bouquet and their fragrance often enhanced those of the flowers accompanying them.

The name *geranium* is a common descriptor used for both the *Geranium* genus of flowers, more commonly known as cranesbills, as well as the *Pelargonium* genus of flowers, more commonly known as geraniums. Both genera are a part of the Geraniaceae family and are respectively named for the resemblance of their seedpods to the water-wading crane and stork. The name *geranium* is derived from the Greek word *geranós* (crane); *pelargonium*, from the Greek word *pelargos* (stork).

SMELL IS IN THE
NOSE OF THE BEHOLDER

One of the unique qualities of the *Pelargonium* is that it can produce a large variety of fragrances that mimic other well-known aromas. There are more than two hundred known varieties of scented-leaved geraniums (always of the *Pelargonium* genera), with the rose geranium being the most popular. Other fragrances these flowers can produce include nutmeg, cinnamon, lemon, strawberry, apple, mint, juniper, and even fish. Yes, it really smells like fish! The list is extensive; all *Pelargonium* genera can be used for cooking, perfume, or potpourri.

The leaves of the cranesbill are edible but sour and bitter tasting, although their flowers can be used as a garnish in salads. Their roots are often used in medicines and herbal remedies, either as a dried powder mixed with water, a poultice that's applied topically, or an ingestible tea made by steeping them in hot water. The leaves and flowers of the *pelargonium* are mild and pleasant tasting and are often used in desserts and salads. Rose geranium is popular for use in jam, simple syrups, and other desserts because of its supposed rose flavor. Lindsey Shere, former executive pastry chef at Alice Waters's restaurant Chez Panisse, shares many floral-based recipes in her cookbook *Chez Panisse Desserts*, including one for rose geranium pound cake.

• ◇ • ◇ • ◇ • ◇ •

*The air was fragrant with the breath of flowers that nodded to
each other from costly vases scattered through both apartments;
and, before one of the windows, rose a bronze stand containing
china jars filled with pelargoniums, in brilliant bloom.*

—AUGUSTA J. EVANS
Vashti; or, Until Death Us Do Part, 1869

HIBISCUS

Hibiscus

Delicate beauty

• ◊ • ◊ •◊• ◊ •

The hibiscus, a flowering plant of the mallow, or Malvaceae family, grows worldwide in warm tropical regions. Native to Africa, Asia, and Europe, the species most commonly referred to in books on the Victorian language of flowers as well as medieval herbals was the *Hibiscus trionum*, also known as Venetian mallow, good-night at noon, or flower of an hour. The reason for these last two names is that the blooms open up only in the morning, last just a few hours before wilting, and drop off by the evening. This makes the flower a great option for garden ornamentation or as a potted plant, but unsuitable for any type of cut-flower arrangement. In addition to this unique blooming habit, its petals can produce an iridescent blue halo lighting effect that is both visible to the human eye and has been shown to increase the foraging efficiency of bees.

According to *Flora's Dictionary*, *Hibiscus trionum* was commonly cultivated in Victorian gardens for "the elegance of its flowers," which are large and cream-colored, with deep-violet or burgundy centers and golden yellow anthers. In an 1885 issue of *The Gardeners' Chronicle*, hibiscus are described as "flowers that you will never forget" and, due to the striking contrast between the creamy-white petals and dark-purple centers, all who see it exclaim, "What an exquisite flower! I must have it!"

Although these flowers seem to have been enjoyed exclusively in the garden, their beauty and symbolism made up for their inability to be used in floral arrangements. The story "The Flower of an Hour, and the Flower Without Fruit," from *Floral Fancies and Morals from Flowers*, is a morality tale that places a personified ranunculus at odds with a personified hibiscus. In the story, the Persian ranunculus, the Flower Without Fruit, is a haughty and beautiful yet empty-hearted flower. It despises her equally beautiful neighbor, a hibiscus, the Flower of an Hour, for her fragility. The ranunculus sees the hibiscus's inability to last the full summer as a shortcoming and expresses this frustration after witnessing a bee take the hibiscus's nectar and happily tell her he will visit her again tomorrow. The hibiscus explains to the ranunculus that her short life has been bright and fulfilled, and after she has died, she will leave behind seeds to supply the next generation of flowers in her place. As autumn arrives, there is nothing left of the ranunculus but a dry stalk, while the hibiscus has left seeds that will sprout again in spring. As spring arrives, the story asks, "Where was now the advantage of her boasted length of days over the Mallow's yet more brief duration?"

In answer, the story asks yet another question, whether a seventy-year-old man who has lived a full life and given back to the world might consider the flower that leaves no fruit more useless than the flower which has contributed to the "economy of creation." In John Gerarde's *The herball, or, Generall historie of plantes*, he writes that the "Adonis flower" described by Ovid in Book X of *Metamorphoses* is thought to describe the "Anemone, or Wind-flower," which would actually be the "quick-fading mallow." Gerarde also writes that when the ancient poet Bion of Smyrna wrote an epitaph to the Greek youth Adonis, he may have unknowingly written an origin story of the *Hibiscus trionum*. Adonis, the mortal lover of Aphrodite, was killed by a boar while hunting. When Aphrodite cried over his body, Bion wrote that a wind-flower (anemone) sprang from the ground where her tears fell. Gerarde believed from Bion's description that the author was mistaken in naming the plant "Wind-flower" and was, in truth, referring to the hibiscus, due to

Georgia O'Keeffe's Hibiscus

In 1939, Georgia O'Keeffe was commissioned to paint the flora and landscapes of Hawaii as part of an advertising campaign for the Dole Pineapple Company. At the end of her nine-week residency, she had produced twenty paintings, including one of her more striking works, *Hibiscus and Plumeria*, a dramatic pink and yellow composition of hibiscus flowers set against a bright blue sky. Unfortunately, none of the paintings from her time spent in Hawaii included a single pineapple, so Dole had the fruit carried by plane to her studio in New York, where she reluctantly completed the job.

---

the flower's fragility and the "matter whereof it sprung, that is a woman's tears, which last not long."

For Victorians, *Hibiscus trionum* represented the romantic aspects of life. In cultures around the world, other varieties of hibiscus have taken on a spiritual meaning. The national flower of South Korea, *Hibiscus syriacus*, sometimes also known as the Korean rose, for instance, is named *mugunghwa*. The Korean word *mugung* means "eternity" and, as South Korea has spent much of its history fighting for its sovereignty, this deepens the flower's significance in their culture. In Hinduism *Hibiscus rosa-sinensis*, a red species of hibiscus, symbolizes the goddess Kali and is given as an offering to her. It is also given as an offering to Lord Ganesha. Hindus believe that hibiscus petals can emit divine consciousness.

The *Hibiscus trionum* is not consumed in foods or medicines. *Hibiscus sabdariffa*, sometimes known as Flor de Jamaica, or Roselle, is a red hibiscus species from West Africa that grows abundantly in China, Thailand, India, Jamaica, Mexico, and Hawaii. It is this species that's commonly used in desserts and beverages. Hibiscus flowers of all varieties continue to be enjoyed in gardens today, with the *Hibiscus trionum* often suggested because it's easy to grow and well suited to country- or cottage-style gardens.

HONEYSUCKLE

Lonicera

Devoted love

• ◇ • ◇ •◇• ◇ •

For the Victorians, honeysuckle was primarily prized for its intoxicating scent and sweet-tasting nectar. According to *The Gardener's Chronicle*, it was cited as an excellent choice for covering unsightly garden walls, arches, or sides of buildings. In *Floral Emblems*, Henry Phillips wrote that the honeysuckle is a happy emblem that "reminds us that sweetness of disposition is a firmer tie than dazzling beauty," and for this reason he gave honeysuckle the symbol of devoted love.

According to the National Records of Scotland, Scottish lore suggested that honeysuckle could help remove freckles and that, if woven into a wreath and placed at the door, it could shield your home from evil and witchcraft. In *Flowers and Flower Lore*, Hilderic Friend writes that the Scottish also used to place branches of honeysuckle in their cowhouses on the second of May to protect them from bewitchment.

Honeysuckle is also known as woodbine, a hardy climbing plant of the Caprifoliaceae family native to the Northern Hemisphere. Its genus, *Lonicera*, was given by Carl Linnaeus in honor of the German Renaissance–era botanist Adam Lonicer, a prolific writer in the fields of botany, arithmetic, and medicine. The vines of honeysuckle shrubs are incredibly tough and known to have been used as rope as early as 2049 BC, in the early Bronze Age.

Henry Lyte wrote that honeysuckle could be found growing everywhere in the English countryside and woods. He also suggested that when added to wine, honeysuckle could help with the hardness and swelling of the spleen and other internal organs, shortness of breath, and to generally purge "the corrupt and evil humours" from the body. He also shared a suggestion by Pedanius Dioscorides to crush honeysuckle leaves in oil and apply directly to bruising caused by illness, ulcers, or other bodily wounds. This oil had the effect of healing wounds and diminishing the appearance of scarring. In today's medicine, certain species of honeysuckle, in particular the *Lonicera japonica*, or Japanese honeysuckle, have been shown to be effective against inflammation and skin infections.

Annie Hassard's *Floral Decorations for the Dwelling House* states that there is no prettier way to decorate a round or oval dinner table than with a "handsome arch" of creeping vines, ferns, and flowers that extends above and over the table setting. She specifically recommends using Japanese honeysuckle as the main focus for such an arch if a greenhouse fern such as the creeping *Lygodium* is unavailable. The arch can then be finished with whatever garden flowers the dinner host may have on hand. Today, flower arches are primarily reserved for special events, such as weddings or large birthday parties and used to decorate doorways or altars both indoors and outside in the garden. Honeysuckles are also still popular in everyday trellis and wall coverings.

The scent and flavor of honeysuckle is often thought of as the perfect signifier for spring and summer, and it can be found in many modern dessert and drink recipes and beauty products. According to the Herbal Academy, honeysuckle is a mild safe herb that can be used by anyone, including children. As a simple syrup it has a light, sweet flavor and can be used as both an alternative to maple syrup or honey, and as a flavoring for drinks. The academy suggests the latter use as an aid for dry scratchy throats. Honeysuckle is also sometimes added to skin creams to help with irritated skin while the online beauty publication Byrdie describes honeysuckle fragrances as "the closest thing we have to bottled sunshine."

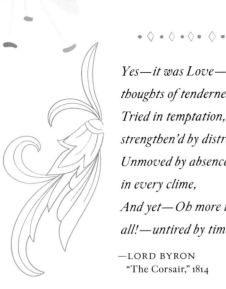

· ◇ · ◇ · ◇ · ◇ ·

Yes—it was Love—if
thoughts of tenderness,
Tried in temptation,
strengthen'd by distress,
Unmoved by absence, firm
in every clime,
And yet—Oh more than
all!—untired by time—

—LORD BYRON
"The Corsair," 1814

SEAHENGE

The prehistoric monument Seahenge, originally located in the village of Holme-next-the-Sea on Holme Beach in Norfolk, England, was made from fifty-five oak trees that had been split into timbers and arranged in a ring formation around a large inverted tree stump. Estimated to have been built during the Bronze Age, it was discovered by a man who had first found a bronze ax in the silt while fishing. When he returned to explore further, he ultimately discovered the upside-down stump. A 1999 excavation unearthed the monument in full, including a length of rope made from honeysuckle vine wrapped through holes in the center tree. Researchers believe this rope would have been used not only to haul the trees to this location, but also to help lower them into the holes they were dug into and to pull them upright.

Seahenge was named by the media in its early days of discovery, and its purpose is still a mystery to researchers today. In an effort to preserve the monument from further seawater damage, it was relocated and reconstructed inside Lynn Museum in the town of King's Lynn, about twenty miles away from Holme Beach. A second henge was discovered on the beach in 2014, but it has been left in place.

HYACINTH

Hyacinthus

Play, game, sport

• ◇ • ◇ • ◇ • ◇ •

he hyacinth is an ancient flower. In fact, one of its earliest mentions in literature is in Homer's *Iliad*. In Book 14, Homer writes that upon seeing his wife, Hera, Zeus is overcome with desire; together they lie down in a bed of flowers made from herbs, violets, lotus, and hyacinth.

In Greek mythology, Hyacinthus was the beautiful young lover of Apollo, the god of music, art, poetry, light, and knowledge. Zephyrus, the West Wind, also admired Hyacinthus and had become jealous that the youth preferred to be with Apollo rather than with him. One day while playing a game of discus with Apollo, Hyacinthus was suddenly struck in the head by the discus and killed. Some versions of the story say that Zephyrus intentionally caused Hyacinthus to be hit, while others say that it was an accident that occurred because Hyacinthus was too eager to impress Apollo. As his lifeless body lay on the ground, his blood pooled out into the grass; the hyacinth grew out of the area where the blood fell. As Apollo mourned for Hyacinthus, his tears fell on the petals of the flower, forever staining it with the sign of his grief. In *Floral Emblems*, Phillips wrote that, because of the hyacinth's relationship to this story, and because of how celebrated the flower had been by ancient poets up to the present day, it appropriately symbolizes play or games.

A fragrant, flowering bulb of the Asparagaceae family that's native to the Mediterranean and related to lily of the valley and asparagus, the hyacinth came to Europe thanks to the renowned French botanist Carolus Clusius. Clusius's friend Ogier Ghiselin de Busbecq was the ambassador to the Ottoman Empire and stationed at the court of Turkish sultan Süleyman I, also called Süleyman the Magnificent. Meanwhile, Clusius was the imperial director of the medical garden in Vienna during the 1570s and 1580s, and Busbecq would frequently send Clusius a variety of bulbs such as tulips, narcissus, and hyacinths. It was common for botanists to share samples of their work with their peers in other countries, and it was from Clusius in Vienna that the hyacinth spread to Brussels and Frankfurt, then throughout Europe, and made its way to England.

At that time, the hyacinth was particularly popular in the southern region of Germany and surrounding areas, but it also grew freely in the fields and pastures of England, especially in western areas. Henry Lyte describes the flower as growing in the colors blue, purple, white, and snow gray, and as having a light and pleasant smell. He also wrote that the hyacinth roots and seeds could be boiled in wine and taken as a diuretic, an aid against oncoming illness, and a remedy for "the venemous bitings of the feeld Spidder."

During the mid-seventeenth century, Madame de Pompadour, official mistress of King Louis XV, is said to have helped establish France as the capital of taste and culture in Europe. Her favorite flower was the hyacinth, and it's been recorded that she ordered that the gardens at Versailles and various other palaces to be filled with them. As she was a prominent trend-setter at the time, her love for the flower sparked a hyacinth craze in France.

According to *The Gardeners' Chronicle* of 1874, Victorians found hyacinths to be "remarkably striking." The flower was popular for both outdoor ornamental gardens as well as indoor cultivation under glass. One reader submitted her opinion that the individual blooms, if mounted on wire, were useful for bouquet making. Supporting this opinion, Annie Hassard writes that a spike of hyacinth, "in its natural state is anything but useful for floral decoration," but if the pips, or individual flowers, were picked off and mounted properly with wire they could be quite versatile. Later in her book she includes them in a buttonhole bouquet arrangement along with a blush-colored rosebud, lily of the valley, and a sprig of fern. She also writes that hyacinths are an appropriate option for spring-themed arrangements. In her chapter on floral wreathes and crosses, which she explains are good offerings to leave on the gravestones of departed friends and relatives, hyacinth pips, along with camellias, snowdrops, and ferns, are included in a large three-foot-wide cross created during the month of February.

Another popular practice in flower cultivation at the time, which may have begun in ancient Rome, was flower forcing, the process by which a flower is forced to produce blooms during its off season. This process was especially common in English gardening as the year-round demand for flowers was high. Hyacinths were considered a good plant for this technique and were often forced to bloom in time for Christmas. In fact, there are many hyacinth bulb-forcing vases produced during the Victorian era that are still available today.

Hyacinths continue to be prized flowers in gardens and bouquets for their versatility, color, and sweet fragrance. Blue or violet hyacinths wouldn't be out of place in a bouquet expressing condolences while white or lighter-hued hyacinths work well for spring or wedding-related occasions.

• ◇ • ◇ • ◇ • ◇ •

It is the Hyacinth, whose sweet bells stooping,
Bend with the odours heavy in their cells;
Amid the shadows of their fragrant drooping,
Memory, that is itself a shadow, dwells.

—LETITIA ELIZABETH LANDON
  "The Hyacinth," *Flowers of Loveliness*, 1837

The Hyacinth Girl

In *The Waste Land* (1922), T. S. Eliot uses the lilac to open the epic poem, and then the hyacinth in the next stanza of the first section, "Book I, the Burial of the Dead." In this part of them poem, he writes about despair and disillusionment, the mixing of old memories and longing amidst new beginnings. He says:

> April is the cruellest month, breeding
> Lilacs out of the dead land, mixing
> Memory and desire, stirring
> Dull roots with spring rain.
> . . . .
> "You gave me hyacinths first a year ago;
> They called me the hyacinth girl."
> —Yet when we came back, late, from the Hyacinth garden,
> Your arms full, and your hair wet, I could not
> Speak, and my eyes failed, I was neither
> Living nor dead, and I knew nothing,
> Looking into the heart of light, the silence.
> *Oed' und leer das Meer.*

It's been suggested that Eliot uses the hyacinth girl to suggest the idealized personal memories of youth, and the hyacinth garden as a reference to sex and breeding, and as a reference to the myth of Apollo and Hyacinth. It's also been suggested that the person with full arms and wet hair is in fact a drowned sailor, as *Oed' und leer das Meer* translates to "desolate and empty the sea," which is a line from the libretto of the opera *Tristan and Isolde*.

Hydrangea

Hydrangea

Boastfulness

• ◇ • ◇ • ◇ • ◇ •

ith fluffy pom-pom-shaped blooms and a soft scent, hydrangeas provide showy ornamentation in the garden. The blooms are not true flowers but leaves with modified colors. The hydrangea is sometimes referred to as the "change rose" because of its ability to change colors based on the pH level of the soil in which it is planted. A soil with higher acidity, for example, usually produces blue or purple leaves, while a more alkaline soil produces pink or red ones. Because hydrangeas produce many large, show-stopping flowers but yield little in seeds and nothing in fruit, they were considered somewhat of a vain or boastful flower by the Victorians. Despite this somewhat negative symbolism, their colors, elaborate appearance, and pleasant fragrance likely helped them maintain a regular presence in the Victorian garden. The fact that they are fairly easy to propagate via cuttings probably also helped with their popularity.

Native to the Western Hemisphere, which includes parts of South and East Asia as well as the Americas, the hydrangea is an ancient flowering shrub of the Hydrangeaceae family. Its name comes from a combination of the Greek words *hydro* (water) and *angeion* (vessel) and may have been given for its cup-shaped seed pods. In modern medicine, hydrangea-leaf extract has been used for a variety of medicinal purposes, ranging from problems with the urinary tract to treatment for malaria. The leaves have been found to contain an alkaloid that is similar to quinine but one hundred times more toxic.

Fossil records indicate that hydrangeas have been growing in the Pacific Northwest since around the late Paleocene to early Eocene epochs (roughly between forty and fifty million years ago), however, none of the ornamental varieties are native to this area. Other hydrangea species fossils that date from the Miocene epoch, roughly between twenty-three and five million years ago, were later recovered in parts of southern China. A shrubby cultivar of wild hydrangea, *Hydrangea arborescens*, grows with small white flowers and is sometimes referred to as "seven barks." It was at times used by the Cherokee Indians and colonial settlers sometime around the seventeenth century as a tea to help with kidney and bladder stones according to *The Dispensatory of the United States of America* by pharmacist Joseph Price Remington. Because vomiting can occur by ingesting this plant, it's believed that the purpose of this tea was to help expel the stones and dissolve any remaining remnants of them. Sometimes the bark would also be chewed for the same effect. Allegedly this treatment worked to great effect for the Cherokee and early settlers but it's inadvisable to try this yourself, as it's also known to cause dizziness, chest pain, and gastrointestinal distress.

The hydrangea first arrived in England when botanist Peter Collinson sent a specimen of *Hydrangea arborescens* back home from Virginia. In volume XIII of *The Botanical Magazine* (1799), William Curtis describes this hydrangea variety as unimpressive but does remark that it's easy to cultivate. Later he says that a "magnificent and highly ornamental variety" of *Hydrangea hortensis* was introduced to Kew Gardens from China in 1790 by Sir Joseph Banks. Curtis described this variety as having "spongy stalks" ranging from one to three feet high, with the younger stalks having purple spots, and large bunches of flowers that would gradate from green to rose as the plant grows.

Soon after its arrival, it was noticed that the type of soil could affect the plant and turn its flowers blue. One reader even wrote to *The Gardeners' Chronicle* of 1841 not only to express how beautiful she found blue hydrangeas, but also to send in samples from her own plant, which had sprouted a sprig of blue flowers, a sprig of pink and red flowers, and another sprig of white and yellow flowers.

In Japan, hydrangeas (*ajisai*) have been cultivated for hundreds of years and are one of five Japanese flowers with a dedicated festival. Bunkyō Ajisai Matsuri (Bunkyō Hydrangea Festival), is held every June through July at the Hakusan Shrine in Bunkyō, Tokyo. This is known as the rainy season (*tsuyu*) in Japan and it's when the hydrangeas are in full bloom. For unknown reasons the Hakusan Shrine has become associated with dental care and, since the Edo period, people have visited to ask the gods for help with tooth problems. Because of this, festivalgoers can also receive free dental information and toothbrushes while viewing the flowers. Other symbols commonly associated with the festival are snails and frogs because of their increased presence during the rainy season. An alternative Japanese name for hydrangea is *nanahenge*, meaning "seven changes," which references the rapid change of costumes by Kabuki performers in some plays and was given for the variety of hues the hydrangea can change into.

In some examples of ancient Japanese art and poetry, the hydrangea was used to support the idea of unresolved romantic situations and an uncertain heart, as can be seen in this passage from twelfth-century poet Fujiwara no Ieyoshi's poem "Fuboku Waka Shō":

> *. . . watching the glow*
> *of flickering fireflies*
> *at twilight*
> *love lingers all the more*
> *in a garden colored by hydrangeas*

The mood of this scene is characterized by unstable elements juxtaposed with stable love: the flickering light of the firefly, the hydrangeas, which change color, and the sun going down. In addition to this, there are some references to the hydrangea being an unpopular garden plant during the Edo period because the samurai saw its ever-changing hues as a symbol of moral unfaithfulness and dishonesty.

Least doers are the greatest boasters.

—WILLIAM GURNALL
The Christian in Complete Armour, 1662

BATHING OF THE BUDDHA

After the Edo period, the popularity of the hydrangea gradually rose, and the plant was more widely cultivated in gardens and temples around Japan. Most hydrangeas are toxic and contain low levels of cyanide; the leaves of the *Hydrangea serrata* and the *Hydrangea macrophylla*, however, contain a natural sweetener. The *Hydrangea serrata* is sometimes referred to as "tea of heaven"; it is characterized as a small and compact shrub with flower clusters that have a lacy appearance versus a fluffy and round one; the *Hydrangea macrophylla* can have either lacy or round flower heads.

Every year in Japan, this sweetener is made into a tea called *amacha*, either by drying the leaves then crushing them into a powder, or by drying the leaves and steeping them whole. This tea is used for the bathing of the Buddha ceremony on April 8, Buddha's alleged birthday. This day is also known as *Hana Matsuri* (Flower Festival) because of how closely it coincides with cherry blossom season and the blooming of other spring flowers. During this ritual, a small statue of Buddha is decorated with flowers in a temple. Participants of the festival can spoon the tea over Buddha as a representation of his birth and of purification. According to the Buddha's Light International Association, participation in this annual custom is said to improve inner balance and harmony and help lead to a more enlightened life. Afterward, the tea is available for drinking, too.

IRIS

Iris

I have a message for you

• ◇ • ◇ • ◇ • ◇ •

ictorians admired the iris but did not cultivate it as frequently as other ornamentals. In *The Gardeners' Chronicle* of 1881, J. Sheppard writes: ". . . except orchids, nothing can be more beautiful in all the floral creation, as they not only have quaintness of form, but the most delicate and rich colours imaginable, and the wonder is they are not more grown than they are, for besides being so showy and effective in borders, they are specially suited for cutting and last a long time in water."

The iris is an ancient flowering bulb of the Iridaceae family, which also includes other beloved blooms such as freesia, gladiolus, and crocus. One of the earliest mentions of the iris was in the writings of Pedanius Dioscorides. The word *iris* is ancient Greek for rainbow, which Dioscorides wrote was given for the flower's resemblance to one: "the flowers on the stalk are bent in one over against another and have varied colours for they are white, pale, black, purple or azure. It is for the variety of colors that it is compared to the heavenly rainbow." In the mythology of ancient Greece, Iris is the personification and goddess of the rainbow as well as a messenger of the gods. In myth, wherever she appears, radiant light and the sweet scent of spring flowers fills the air. In *Plant Lore, Legends, and Lyrics*, Richard Folkard writes

that the Greeks placed irises on tombs "possibly because the goddess Iris was believed to guide the souls of dead women to their last resting-place, as Mercury conducted the souls of men."

Irises, sometimes previously known as "floure Deluces" or "garden flagges" in older texts, have grown freely in Europe for many centuries. According to Henry Lyte's *A niewe Herball*, there were multiple varieties that ranged in size, color, and habitat, growing freely near rivers, lakes, and in the lowland country-side throughout England. The roots, flowers, and leaves of some blue or purple varieties were used in the production of fabric dye. Iris roots were employed for a range of medicinal purposes, too. The juice of the green roots was used as a a diuretic; its effectiveness was due to the plant's toxicity. When the juice was mixed with honey, it was considered as an aid to suppress coughing and relieve shortness of breath. This same mixture was often applied topically to relieve ulcerated or chafed skin, and even on the face to diminish the appearance of freckles and blemishes. Lyte also believed that consuming a combination of the juice from the root with water and vinegar helped alleviate the pain from insect stings. He also advised anointing the forehead with a mixture of the juice and rose oil to relieve headaches.

Today, irises are no longer used for medicinal purposes and can be found more commonly in perfumes and aromatherapy oils. Nonetheless, a recent study at University of Florida Center for Aquatic and Invasive Plants reported that yellow irises are sometimes planted to help with water purifi-cation because their roots are able to absorb pollutants. This study described success with transplanting the iris from is natural habitat of wetlands and marshes, into "well-watered" gardens around the world for the treatment of sewage and to remove metals such as copper from wastewaters.

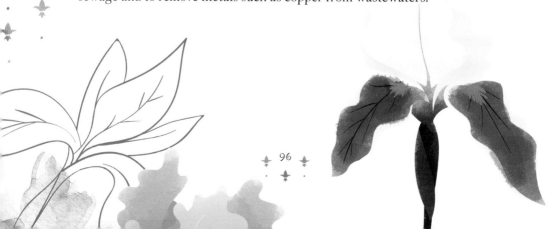

FLEUR-DE-LIS

The fleur-de-lis has been used to represent a variety of entities throughout the ages, particularly royal houses and religious orders. One of the earliest religious legends regarding its origin is the story of Clovis (c. AD 466 to c. 511–513), king of the Franks, and his conversion to Christianity. His wife, Saint Clotilda, had long prayed for him to convert from paganism to Christianity, but he resisted. Later, after leading his armies in a prolonged battle against the Huns, and facing imminent defeat, Clovis desperately turned to the God of his wife for help and soon after, the battle turned in his favor. Owing this victory to his wife's God, he had himself baptized. Saint Clotilda had previously shared a vision with him that the three toads in the arms of France had been replaced by three lilies, so he chose to represent these on his shield during his baptism. Another version of this story writes that Clovis was shown the lilies by the Virgin Mary.

Although the French word *fleur-de-lis* translates as "flower of the lily," the symbol is a stylized depiction of an iris that has been used by French kings as an emblem of their supremacy for many centuries. The fleur-de-lis has long been depicted in flags, shields, and architecture, however King Louis VII (1120–1180) was the first king to use it as his official symbol, and had it emblazoned on his shield and royal banners. Folkard writes in *Plant Lore, Legends, and Lyrics* (1884), that *fleur-de-lis* was originally *fleur de Louis*, which was later changed to *fleur de Luce*, and finally *fleur de lys*, or *lis*. Further elaborating on the origin as Louis's flower, Folkard writes that in 1137, while engaged in the Second Crusade, Louis had seen the iris in a dream and, for this reason, adopted it as his emblem. It's also thought by some researchers that *lys* or *lis* could be a corruption of Loys, an alternative spelling for the names Clovis, Louis, and Lois that was commonly used by French kings until the time of Louis XIII, who became king of France in 1610.

The later reduction of using only three fleur de lis symbols on the French coat of arms was allegedly the work of the French king Charles V, who in 1376 chose to honor the holy trinity of God as three beings: the Father, the Son, and the Holy Spirit.

Jasmine

Jasminum

WHITE: Amiability
YELLOW: Grace and elegance

• ◇ • • ◇ • ◇ • ◇ •

n John Claudius Loudon's *Arboretum et Fruticetum Britannicum* (1838)*,* a botanical guide to the trees and shrubs of England, he recounts a well-known yet anonymously sourced legend related to the custom of brides wearing jasmine in their hair on their wedding day. Loudon's story was frequently published in Victorian gardening magazines. There isn't any evidence that it actually occurred, but the story goes that in 1699, a certain unnamed grand duke of Tuscany owned a fine specimen of the yellow *Jasminum odoratissimum* from Goa, seemingly the only jasmine plant in the kingdom. He was so proprietary about the propagation of his beloved jasmine that he forbade anyone else from growing it.

The duke happened to employ a personal gardener. The fellow was in love with a local peasant girl and, as a token of his affection, took a single sprig from the plant and gave it to her for her birthday. The girl planted the sprig; it grew so large so quickly that her neighbors began to drop by to admire the exotic flower with the lovely scent, even paying her for their own sprigs to plant. Without the duke's knowledge, the girl eventually raised enough money from selling the jasmine sprigs that she and the gardener were able to marry. Loudon concludes, "the young girls of Tuscany, in remembrance of this adventure, always deck themselves, on their wedding-day, with a

nosegay of jessamine," and that there is also a Tuscan proverb that says, "she who is worthy to wear a nosegay of jessamine, is as good as a fortune to her husband." He shares that this custom apparently made its way to the brides of Yemen as well.

There is a cultivar of jasmine from southern Asia and India called *Jasminum sambac*, which is sometimes referred to as the Duke of Tuscany, or Arabian jasmine. This is a white, very full, double-petaled variety similar in appearance to a carnation, and it has a loose connection to the story through its name and country of origin. Belle of India is another double-petaled variety of the *Jasminum sambac* that is less full looking, but there is no indication that it is related to the lore.

Jasmine is considered one of India's most beautiful and fragrant native flowers. It plays an important role in weddings, religious ceremonies, and festivals. It is used to frame the entrances of temples around the country, as

JASMINE-SCENTED TEA

The Chinese city of Fuzhou is famous for having the most favorable climate to grow many species of jasmine. It is also the place where the method for scenting tea was invented. Traditionally, the process of scenting tea involved plucking jasmine blossoms first thing in the morning after they'd opened, then layering them with already prepared and processed tea leaves. Over the course of several weeks the jasmine continued to release its fragrance, which was absorbed by the leaves.

In Fuzhou, jasmine tea is considered an antidote to many kinds of poison and is incorporated into herbal medicines. According to the Food and Agricultural Organization of the United Nations, in the Fuzhou dialect, the word for buying medicine literally means "buying tea"; the word for brewing medicine means "brewing tea"; and the word for taking medicine means "drinking tea."

incense in *puja* (prayer) rooms, to adorn a bride's hair on her wedding day, or to flavor or garnish wedding dishes. It's thought that the tradition of wearing jasmine started as a method of perfuming the hair and body, yet the flower has come to be associated with symbols of prosperity and good fortune. In Hindu worshipping practices, many gods and deities have specific flowers associated with them that are considered acceptable offerings, with jasmine being one of the few that is acceptable as an offering for all.

According to *The Folklore of Plants*, popular European lore says that if one sees jasmine in a dream, it is a good omen.

After the rose, jasmine is the world's most popular flower, beloved for its beauty, exquisite fragrance, and flavoring in desserts and drinks. In Chinese culture, jasmine symbolizes "forever love" and is one of the holy flowers used in Buddhism. It's thought that the fragrance of jasmine is the scent of heaven.

Jasmine is an old genus of climbing shrubs and vines of the very large Oleaceae family, which includes other well-known plant species such as lilac and olive trees. Jasmine is native to the tropical climates of Europe, Africa, and Asia, in areas that are considered part of the Old World. During the Western Han dynasty (206 BC–AD 9), jasmine was imported to China from the Persian Gulf, where it was first cultivated for scenting tea. Later, during the Qing dynasty (1636–1912), machine production of jasmine-scented tea made it possible to more easily export it to Western countries.

As an indigenous plant, jasmine has been popular and commonly planted in English gardens for many centuries. In the Victorian era, it was considered an elegant plant that would "perfume the air to a great distance with its delicious fragrance," according to *Flora's Dictionary*. Henry Lyte suggested applying the flowers topically to help with red spots or swelling of the skin, and to use the oil to help with headaches.

In an excerpt from *The Art of Perfumery* (1857), George Septimus writes that jasmine "is one of the most prized by the perfumer. Its odor is delicate and sweet, and so peculiar that it is without comparison, and as such cannot be imitated." He goes on to explain how perfumers obtained the jasmine scent through enfleurage, whereby a mixture of "pure lard and suet" is spread over a glass tray, "and sticking the fresh gathered flowers all over it, leaving them to stand a day or so, and repeating the operation with fresh flowers— the grease absorbs the odor." This mixture, then referred to as a pomade, or pomatum, is then scraped off the tray, melted, and strained. Another method for obtaining the scent was to dip balls of wool in oil, then repeatedly cover with fresh jasmine flowers. The balls were then squeezed through a press to create jasmine oil. Any of the pomade or oil that wasn't used in the creation of a liquid perfume was reserved for use as a balm for the hair and skin.

Victorians often scented their handkerchiefs, using them to shield themselves from any disagreeable odors they might encounter while out in public. Septimus notes that jasmine perfume was one of the "great many of the most approved handkerchief perfumes sold by the English and French perfumers." If jasmine was used in too pure a form it could be overwhelming and sickly; however, he notes that if it is "judiciously mixed with other perfumes of an opposite character [it] is sure to please the most fastidious customer."

• ◊ • ◊ • ◊ • ◊ •

From plants that wake when others sleep,
From timid jasmine buds, that keep
Their odour to themselves all day,
But, when the sun-light dies away,
Let the delicious secret out
To every breeze that roams about.

—THOMAS MOORE
Lalla Rookh: The Light of the Haram, 1817

LAVENDER

Lavandula

Distrust

• ◇ • ◇ • ◇ • ◇ •

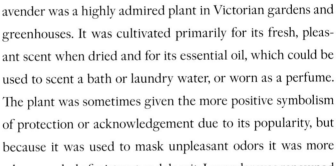

avender was a highly admired plant in Victorian gardens and greenhouses. It was cultivated primarily for its fresh, pleasant scent when dried and for its essential oil, which could be used to scent a bath or laundry water, or worn as a perfume. The plant was sometimes given the more positive symbolism of protection or acknowledgement due to its popularity, but because it was used to mask unpleasant odors it was more widely recognized as a symbol of mistrust and deceit. Lavender was renowned for a variety of medicinal and therapeutic qualities such as helping with relaxation or treating cuts and burns. More recent studies have shown it to be effective as a mood stabilizer and for treating nervous system problems. Because of its beauty, fragrance, and ease of cultivation, it remains popular today.

Lavender flowers and leaves have long been enjoyed in a variety of desserts, savory dishes, and drinks. It's been said that Queen Elizabeth I would drink lavender tea as medicinal treatment to ease her migraines but that she also loved the taste so much that she ordered that her table always be set with lavender jam.

Lavender is an ancient flowering plant of the Lamiaceae, or mint family, that's native to the Mediterranean. The name *lavender* comes from the Latin word *lavare* meaning "to wash." Some of the earliest records indicate that lavender was commonly used by the Romans and in medieval Europe

to scent the water for washing clothes and bathing. The expressions "laid up in lavender" and "laid out in lavender," both refer to the cleanliness associated with the scent, but in different ways. The first refers to storing clothes with lavender to preserve them well and to protect them from insects such as moths. While laying someone out in lavender refers to dressing a corpse in burial dress, the reference to lavender refers to the custom of strewing lavender or other herbs near the deceased to mask the smell.

In addition to warding off odor, lavender was used to ward off evil or sorcery. In *The Folklore of Plants*, T. F. Dyer writes that, in Tuscany, lavender could help protect a potential victim from an evil eye, a type of malevolent curse that can cause illness and bad luck. In a more material scenario, lavender possesses antimicrobial properties and is known to be effective in warding off harmful bacteria that would negatively affect medical procedures. In ancient Egypt, lavender essential oil was one of many herbal plant oils commonly included in the process of cleaning and preserving bodies for mummification because it was inexpensive and readily available, and its antimicrobial qualities helped maintain the proper conditions for the practice.

In his book *A History of Egyptian Mummies*, surgeon Thomas Joseph Pettigrew wrote that lavender was often used in modern mummifications. Specifically, he recounts that the renowned surgeon William Hunter, professor of anatomy at the Royal Academy of Arts in London from 1769 to 1772, had a method of embalming that he would often include in his lectures. The process started with a mixture of Venice turpentine, oil of chamomile, and oil of lavender, all used for antiseptic purposes. This fluid was then colored with vermillion and forced into the large arteries of a cadaver where it would sit for many hours so that it could be fully absorbed by the body. Following this was a series of repeated steps of draining and pumping the body with the mixture after removing the internal organs and bathing all surfaces with "camphorated spirits of wine." With the final draining step completed, a powder made from camphor, resin, and niter was dusted over all surfaces and cavities of the body. The oils of rosemary and lavender would then be rubbed over the body, and it would be placed in a cast made from plaster of paris to remove all remaining moisture. This cast was a type of coffin that was not to be opened for at least four years.

One of Hunter's more interesting specimens that had been prepared with this same method involving lavender was Mary, the departed wife of an eccentric English dentist, Martin van Butchell. According to Pettigrew, a newspaper that had been held at the Royal College of Surgeons contained an account of the embalming events written in van Butchell's own words. The dentist wrote that his wife had died at 2:30 AM, the morning of January 14, 1775. By 8 AM, a plaster cast had been taken of her face and at 2:30 PM her body was receiving the first injections of the embalming fluid by Hunter and his assisting doctors. After being laid in the plaster coffin, the body was repeatedly washed and treated with oils including lavender, at Hunter's direction.

In 1803, the Royal College of Surgeons of England published a book, *Life and Character of the Celebrated Mr. Martin Van Butchell*, which said that the dentist had such a deep affection for Mary that he was at first determined to never bury her, which was why after the embalming, she was kept for an extended period of time in her wedding dress, fixed up with glass eyes, injected with carmine, which made her skin appear rosy, and kept in a glass case in his sitting room. The college writes that he often had visitors "in great numbers of the nobility and gentry," however they felt van Butchell was intentionally making his wife into a show and frequently expressed their disagreement with the situation. The college also shares that some believed van Butchell did this because of a clause in his marriage settlement that stipulated "disposing of certain property while she remained above ground," however this fact remained unsubstantiated. According to Eric Jameson's *The Natural History of Quackery*, van Butchell eventually remarried and his new wife demanded that Mary be moved out. Mary was taken to the museum of the Royal College of Surgeons in London, where she was housed for 150 years until her corpse was destroyed in a German bombing raid in 1941.

BLUE GOLD AND WHITE FLOWERS

Provence's temperate climate—hot summers, moderate winters, and just the right amount of sun and rain—have made it one of the most hospitable environments for growing some of the world's most fragrant flowers. Roses, jasmine, tuberose, orange blossom, violet, mimosa, narcissus, and lavender all thrive there. In fact, more than half of the world's fine lavender exports come from France, although, at one point, when the flower was hard to find, locals referred to it as "blue gold"—and the name stuck.

If you travel to Provence in the summer, you'll very likely find yourself enveloped by lavender's pleasant aroma, as fluffy rolling hills of the deep purple flower are in bloom across the entire landscape from mid-June through August. The medieval village of Sault, situated on a hilltop at the heart of the region, with dense acres of lavender and lavandin fields extending in every direction, is a main area of lavender production. The Fête de la Lavande (Lavender Festival) is held here every August, and the town is a main stop on the official Lavender Route, a tour through the key areas where lavender is produced and distilled. The region's primary export is lavender oil, which is used in perfume and for aromatherapy. The oil comes primarily from lavandin, a hybrid between true lavender (*Lavendula augustifolia*) and spike lavender (*Lavendula latifolia*). Lavandin is known to have a stronger, sweeter scent than true lavender and is easier to cultivate, although in perfumery it's considered to be of lower quality than true lavender.

Closer to the coast, in the hills above Cannes is the town of Grasse, which has been considered the perfume capital of the world for more than five hundred years. The region's Mediterranean climate has long made it a main supplier of many flower varieties used in iconic fragrances. The jasmine and roses in Chanel No. 5, arguably the world's most iconic perfume, are grown exclusively here in fields at an estate that has supplied the couture house singularly for decades. Chanel's rival, Dior, has an exclusive arrangement with another local cultivator for the roses and jasmine that go into its perfumes. Also in Grasse is the International Perfume Museum, which houses rare antique fragrance jars and perfumery tools, and a botanical garden filled with fragrant cultivars arranged by their olfactory notes and available for the pleasure of your taking them in.

LILAC

Syringa

PURPLE: The first emotions of love
WHITE: Youthful innocence

• ◇ • ◇ • ◇ • ◇ •

t's believed that lilacs were first introduced to Western Europe around 1563 by Ogier Ghiselin de Busbecq, the Flemish ambassador to the Ottoman Empire, who had returned from Constantinople at the end of his service with many foreign plant varieties. *The Lilac* by botanist Susan McKelvey explains that it's not known for certain when the common lilac was first successfully cultivated in Europe, but she suggests that it was either in Busbecq's garden in Flanders, or in the garden of Busbecq's friend Carolus Clusius in Vienna. It appears that the lilac may have been growing in both gardens around the same time, but it's unknown which plant grew first. From there, the lilac spread throughout the rest of Europe, likely from Clusius sharing his samples with friends in other countries, a common practice. By 1629 the lilac was well established in English gardens. McKelvey also writes that the lilac didn't arrive in America until 1904 when E. T. Williams sent seeds to the Arnold Arboretum of Harvard University. According to the arboretum, lilacs were so popular and frequently cultivated by French nurserymen that France became synonymous with fine lilacs.

Lilacs were originally known as *Philadelphus*, supposedly after the Egyptian king Ptolemy Philadelphus; however, the *Philadelphus* is a separate plant that ancient records seem to have confusingly categorized with the

lilac under the genus *Syringa*. In any event, lilacs have been known as *Syringa* since at least 1576 when Clusius and the botanist Mathias de Lobel recorded them as such. The botanist Carl Linnaeus was the first to formally describe the flower in book form, *Species Plantarum*, and officially name it *Syringa*, derived from the Greek word *suriggos* meaning "pipe" or "flute." Linnaeus was inspired by Clusius's account that explained that the Turks had a practice of clearing the pith from the tubular branches of the lilac so they could use them as tobacco pipes. McKelvey shares a small bit of Greek mythology from Ovid's *Metamorphoses* that tells the story of Syrinx, a nymph of Arcady, who was being pursued through the woods by the Greek satyr Pan. Pan changed her into a reed and from this he constructed the world's first pan flute.

The flower colors range from a very light, almost white, purple to dark mauve, making this an attractive ornamental flower. Because of its appearance and intoxicating scent, it was commonly found in the Victorian garden and often used in forced cultivation for out-of-season decorative purposes. In Annie Hassard's *Floral Decorations for the Dwelling House*, she suggests Christmas table decorations consisting of a bed of fern and ivy fronds set in the bottom of a round dish, then topped with white chrysanthemums, scarlet pelargoniums, holly berries, laurustinus, and white lilacs.

For the sweetest, wisest soul of all my days and lands . . .
and this for his dear sake;
Lilac and star and bird twined with the chant of my soul,
There in the fragrant pines and the cedars dusk and dim.

—WALT WHITMAN
"When Lilacs Last in the Door-Yard Bloom'd," *Leaves of Grass*, 1865

A Scent of Lilac
Breathing from the Hedge

The bridesmaids' eight bouquets of white lilac and lilies of the valley had been sent in due time, as well as the gold and sapphire sleeve-links of the eight ushers and the best man's cat's-eye scarf-pin; Archer had sat up half the night trying to vary the wording of his thanks for the last batch of presents from men friends and ex-lady-loves; the fees for the Bishop and the Rector were safely in the pocket of his best man; his own luggage was already at Mrs. Manson Mingott's, where the wedding-breakfast was to take place, and so were the travelling clothes into which he was to change; and a private compartment had been engaged in the train that was to carry the young couple to their unknown destination—concealment of the spot in which the bridal night was to be spent being one of the most sacred taboos of the prehistoric ritual.

—EDITH WHARTON
The Age of Innocence, 1920

American novelist and playwright Edith Wharton (1862–1937) was renowned for her stories, which served as commentary on the manners and morals of upper-class New York society in the late nineteenth century, but she was also an accomplished interior decorator, gardener, and landscape designer. After purchasing The Mount, her estate in Lenox, Massachusetts, in 1901, she began to design the property's outdoor spaces with inspiration from garden designs she encountered on her many trips abroad. Particularly influenced by gardens in England, France, and Italy, she aspired to create a series of elegant outdoor rooms that would serve as a harmonious extension of the interior of her house with tree- and flower-lined walkways connecting each of these areas. Lilac trees were featured prominently in her garden, so when the Edith Wharton Restoration undertook a full reclamation in 2001, sixty Meyer lilacs were planted in accordance with her original garden designs.

LILY

Lilium

WHITE: Purity and sweetness
YELLOW: Falsehood

• ◇ • ◇ • ◇ • ◇ •

An ancient flowering bulb of the Liliaceae, or lily family, native to temperate regions of the Northern Hemisphere, the lily is one of the oldest known and cultivated plants, with evidence of the Madonna lily being used for ornamentation, medicinal ointments, and food in Asia Minor during the second millennium BC. It's thought that the yellow lily may have originated in Persia and that the ancient Persian capital, Susa, or Shushan, may be the source of its name. The name *Susa* may derive from the protective Elamite god Inshushinak, although it's possible that the name comes from *Ŝuŝan*, the Persian translation of the biblical Hebrew name *Shoshannah*, which in biblical times meant "lily." Today, the name *Shoshannah* more often refers to the rose. In ancient Persian poetry, the lily and its leaves have been likened to a tongue, a sword, and a dagger.

In Roman mythology, the lily was said to be one of goddess Juno's favorite flowers and was given to her as an offering in ceremonies. Roman mythology also put forth that the original color of the lily was the color of a purple crocus, but Juno, having dropped some milk on the earth, changed its color to white. In *A niewe Herball*, there is a lily origin story written by the Roman emperor, Constantine. The god Jupiter has fathered a son with a human woman, Alcumena. In an attempt to make his half-mortal infant son Hercules fully immortal, Jupiter takes the baby to the breast of his sleeping wife, Juno. After it seemed that Hercules had taken enough milk, Jupiter carried him away and, as he did, drops of milk fell across the skies, forming the Milky Way. From the drops that fell to earth, sprang milk-white lilies. Henry Lyte also wrote that white lilies grew indigenously and were commonly cultivated in English gardens in the sixteenth century. He writes that the bulb could be used both topically and internally to treat a variety of ailments such as "corruption of the blood," aching joints, burns, or snake bites.

The plant family Liliaceae is called "the lily family," however only those from the *Lilium* genus are considered true lilies by botanists. The daylily and calla lily, for example, are unrelated to each other or to the *Lilium* genus, and are commonly confused for true lilies due their names and similar appearance. The bright pink stargazer lily (*Lilium orientalis* "Stargazer") and white and yellow royal lily (*Lilium regale*) are examples of true lily varieties.

Lilies were highly sought after by Victorian-era explorers and botanists, who often journeyed from England and North America to find exotic plants. Such expeditions were common at the time, as gardening and cultivating plants was popular, both indoors iand out. One explorer in particular, the Irish plantsman Augustine Henry, diligently explored central and southwestern China, amassing a large collection of native plant specimens. Among these samples was an orange lily that was sent to Kew Gardens in London in 1889. This species became known as the Henry lily, sometimes called the tiger lily, and is still cultivated worldwide. Those who love J. M. Barrie's *Peter Pan* (1904) are no doubt familiar with the name *Tiger Lily*, used for Neverland's princess.

Because lilies represent purity, they have long been a part of wedding ceremonies. In T. F. Dyer's *The Folklore of Plants*, he mentions that lilies and roses were commonly entwined in what he calls the "bridal garland," garlands of flowers used for decorating walkways, doorways, arches, and all general areas of a wedding party. Some European countries hold the superstition that if a man tramples on a lily, he will crush the purity of the womenfolk of his

household. The specific origin of this myth isn't given, although Dyer mentions that in Italy, the lily (especially white) and the rose were closely tied to the Virgin Mary: "the pure white petals signifying her spotless body, and the golden anthers within typifying her soul sparkling with divine light." Today, white lilies remain a popular choice for bridal bouquets and decorations as well as arrangements to express condolences or to celebrate spring holidays.

CONSIDER THE LILIES OF THE FIELD

In Christianity, the lily is most often associated with the Virgin Mary as it symbolizes purity, although it's also frequently tied to Solomon, King of Israel and Judah, as a biblical symbol of physical beauty and splendor. The lily is mentioned numerous times in the Bible, but the most occurrences appear in the Song of Songs, or Song of Solomon, a book of the Old Testament that celebrates sexual intimacy through a collection of love poems. To support this, references to Solomon and the lily are found in other parts of the Old Testament. In Sermon on the Mount (Matthew 6:28), where the primary discussion is the concern about material possessions, Jesus tells his followers: "And why are ye anxious concerning raiment? Consider the lilies of the field, how they grow; they toil not, neither do they spin: yet I say unto you, that even Solomon in all his glory was not arrayed like one of these."

According to John Pople's *The King Who Fell*, this mention of Solomon in the context of lilies associates him with the idea of the lily as an object of physical beauty. Pople gives another example from the Old Testament in the Book of Kings (7:19), where it's mentioned that Solomon has added lilies to the tops of the pillars in his temple, which had been originally designed by his father, David. David's temple had no lilies, and Solomon's addition of them was purely for decoration. Because the lilies have been placed in a *capital* position, as caps for the tops of the pillars, Pople suggests that Solomon has a weakness for beautiful things and places a high value on them, which strengthens his tie to the lily as a symbol of beauty.

LILY OF THE VALLEY

Convallaria majalis

Return of happiness

• ◇ • ◇ •◇• ◇ •

lthough the rose was one of the favorite flowers of French fashion designer Christian Dior, it was lily of the valley that he cherished the most. It adorned his personal stationery, the lapels of his jackets and his fashion designs, and inspired his 1954 spring collection. He even stitched a lily of the valley on the inside of linings or hems, and he made sure that at least one model in every show was wearing a little bunch of the flower. It's been said that he was superstitious and believed the lily of the valley to be a holy and lucky flower. In 1956, the Dior fragrance Diorissimo—with lily of the valley as one of its heart notes—was created in his honor. Today, this fragrance remains one of the most realistic approximations of the scent of lily of the valley and, according to the Christian Dior company, it is "the scented expression of [Dior's] soul." Coincidentally, that same year, when actress Grace Kelly married Prince Rainier of Monaco, she carried a small bouquet of lilies of the valley.

The lily of the valley is a flowering woodland plant of the Asparagaceae family, which also contains the genera *Hyacinth* and *Asparagus*, and is native to the Northern Hemisphere in Asia and Europe. It is an extremely toxic

plant with a strong, sweet smell, and its small, white bell-shaped flowers grow on tall curved stems. The plant primarily produces white blossoms, but there are more rare cultivars that may have blooms with a slight pink or purple tint to them. Despite the plant's toxicity, it was used in small doses for a variety of medicinal purposes. Lily of the valley, referred to in Henry Lyte's *A niewe Herball* as the "May Lillie" and "Lillie Conuall," could help with memory loss if "the water of the flouers" was distilled "with a good strong wine" and taken one spoonful at a time. It was also said that drops of the same liquid applied directly to the eye could help with inflammation.

According to T. F. Dyer's *Folklore of Plants*, a medieval superstition originating in Devonshire, England, held that it was considered unlucky to plant a bed of lily of the valley and that anyone who did so would die within twelve months, but clearly it didn't carry much weight. Victorians considered lily of the valley an exquisite flower, both in form and aroma, that announced the joyous advent of spring—thus its association with the return of happiness. Annie Hassard's *Floral Decorations for the Dwelling House* suggests including lily of the valley—along with pale-colored pelargonium and maidenhair fern in the top dish of a multitiered arrangement that might be used for a large dinner party setting in the month of March. Other suggested arrangements include mixing them with scarlet begonias for Christmas Day, with white azaleas and cyclamens for a breakfast table setting, or with purple *Dendrobium nobile* orchids in a small vase for a drawing room. The book further recommends using them in a spring mantlepiece decoration with tulips and hyacinths or as a single sprig in a buttonhole bouquet with any color rosebud.

MAY DAY

In France, May Day is a public holiday that has been celebrated since May 1, 1561, when it is said that King Charles IX was given a bunch of lilies of the valley as a token of luck and prosperity for the coming year. The king liked the sweet-smelling gift so much that he began the custom of giving the flowers to the ladies of his court. At the turn of the twentieth century, it became customary for a man to give a lily-of-the-valley bouquet to his beloved. Today, the flowers are given to good friends and family members as a general token of affection. Giving someone a lily-of-the-valley sprig is also akin to wishing them luck.

The French once had an old tradition of holding *bals de muguets* (lily-of-the-valley dances), where once a year, boys and girls would meet without getting their parents' permission first. It was customary for the girls to wear white and for the boys to wear a sprig of lily of the valley as a boutonniere.

May 1 is also considered Labor Day in France, a day of action inspired by an American strike in Chicago in 1889. At first, French May Day protesters wore a red triangle pin, with each of the three sides representing the ideal division of the day: equal parts work, leisure, and sleep. Today, a small bouquet of lily of the valley tied with a red ribbon has replaced the pin.

• ◊ • ◊ • ◊ • ◊ •

And the Naiad-like lily of the vale,

Whom youth makes so fair and passion so pale

That the light of its tremulous bells is seen

Through their pavilions of tender green.

—PERCY BYSSHE SHELLEY
"The Sensitive Plant," 1820

original Diorissimo bottle

LOTUS

Nelumbo nucifera

Silence

• ◊ • ◊ • ◊ • ◊ •

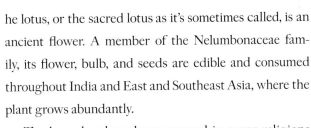

The lotus, or the sacred lotus as it's sometimes called, is an ancient flower. A member of the Nelumbonaceae family, its flower, bulb, and seeds are edible and consumed throughout India and East and Southeast Asia, where the plant grows abundantly.

The lotus has long been revered in many religions and cultures worldwide. Virtually every Hindu god or goddess is portrayed sitting atop a lotus with a lotus in hand. Because the lotus opens during the day and closes at night, it is a symbol of rebirth and creation, in addition to silence. Ancient Hindu scriptures contain many creation myths that tell of the birth of Brahmā, the creator of the universe. These often involve some variation of his being born, fully formed, from a lotus flower. In one story, it's said that he was born as the universe was forming from the blossom of a lotus flower, which grew from the navel of Lord Vishnu as he lay floating on water, lost in prayer.

In *Indian Mythology* (1917), Arthur Keith writes that the Buddhist scripture *Saṃyutta Nikāya* often makes direct connections between Gautama Buddha (c. 563–480 to c. 483–400 BC), the monk on whose teachings Buddhism was founded, and the lotus (*Nelumbo nucifera*). The scripture says, "As the lotus grows up in the water from which it is born, rises above it, and ceases to be sullied by it, thus the Buddha grows above the world and is no longer defiled by it." Buddha is frequently depicted sitting atop a lotus throne in ancient and modern artworks.

If they found a culture outside Europe to be exotic, Victorians often romanticized and Westernized it, adapting it to make it their own. The opening of trade to Japan and China resulted in a great cultural influence—referred to as Orientalism with reference to art and design in particular—in nineteenth-century Europe and the United States. In 1838, American businessman Nathan Dunn opened the Chinese Museum in Philadelphia; in conjunction with the event, he published a 120-page catalog, *Ten Thousand Chinese Things*. The exhibition drew one hundred thousand visitors and an equal number in London, where the collection was displayed in 1842, just as the British were signing a trade treaty with China. According to the Victoria and Albert Museum, "it was the most comprehensive show yet seen of Chinese material culture—as well as decorative arts and paintings and architectural models. . . . The exhibition . . . remained open for years." Although the exhibition may have increased knowledge about China, the standard (and patronizing) perceptions that Americans and English people held regarding Chinese culture remained unchanged. The same Westernization took place when the London International Exhibition of 1862 presented Japanese material culture in large number to a wide audience for the first time.

Due to the British colonization of India, Buddhism was also heavily subjected to Orientalism. Victorians were fascinated by spiritual issues surrounding life and death, as they began to move away from traditional Christian practices, replacing faith in God with science. The belief in the soul's eternal life and the regular attendance of church declined, and Victorians increasingly turned toward other religions, cultures, and forms of mysticism for answers to their existential questions. Buddhism was one of these outlets; Egyptology and its connections to the occult and spirituality was another.

Victorians had difficulty relating to most traditional Hindu practices. They found Hindu spiritualism and deities to be overly imaginative and childish, and its practices of meditation and contemplation lazy. The figure of Buddha, however, presented them with an important opportunity for large-scale influence. The Victorians romanticized Buddha, recontextualizing him in relation to the Bible, making him less divine and more human. Serious Victorian interest in Buddhism began around the 1830s, and by the 1860s it had matured into a viable religion. Somewhere between the late 1870s and early 1880s, the Victorian Buddha became a model for the "ideal Victorian gentleman" and, ultimately, a tool for asserting control to create social reforms in India. As people came to question the Bible and its non-historically based cosmological ideas, Buddha was reinvented as more of a spiritual entity, yet one who was still aligned with the Victorian guidelines for morality.

In Egyptian lore, the lotus was also considered a symbol of rebirth and creation because every morning it rose to the surface of the water and opened its petals to the sun. In some versions of an old Egyptian creation story, the sun god Ra was born from a blue lotus bud. It's for these reasons that Ra, as well as the god of the underworld, Osiris, were frequently depicted holding a lotus or in the presence of the flowers.

This lotus, however, was later identified as being one of two varieties of water lily, either the Egyptian white lily (*Nymphaea lotus*) or the Egyptian blue lily (*Nymphaea caerulea*). Although unrelated to the lotus Hindus favored, the water lily's Egyptian iconography is similar to that of Hinduism's sacred lotus, and these lilies were often mistakenly or interchangeably referred to as lotuses in Victorian texts. As a decorative motif, the Egyptian lotus was woven into all elements of Egyptian art, architecture, and rituals. In fact, when King Tut's Tomb was discovered, archeologists found that he had been buried with a necklace made of a variety of flowers that included blue lotus.

Classical Greek and Roman mythology were also highly referenced in the art and literature favored by well-educated Victorians. The Egyptian god Horus, for example, was adapted by the Greeks and renamed Harpocrates. Harpocrates was the Greek god of silence, secrets, and confidentiality and was often depicted sitting on a lotus flower. It was for this reason that Henry Phillips's *Floral Emblems* assigns the lotus the meaning of silence. Add to this the co-opting of Hindu and Egyptian cultures for design and symbolism, and it's easy to see how the lotus would have been meaningful for the Victorians from an aesthetic and spiritual point of view. Depictions of the lotus can often be found in Victorian architectural details such as columns and fountains in gardens and cemeteries.

By most accounts, the sacred lotus (*Nelumbo nucifera*) was the Victorians' species of choice and cultivated primarily by the wealthy, those who owned large grounds and could afford to maintain a pond. In an 1895 issue of *The Gardeners' Chronicle*, the obituary for W. S. Kimball, a wealthy American orchidist, describes the collections he left behind including his lily house, "a unique feature, with its long oval pond, edged with Papyrus, and covered with water-lilies—the *Nymphaea zanzibariensis*, the Lotus, and the splendid *Victoria Regia*." In 1852, Kew Gardens constructed its Waterlily House, designing it specially to showcase all tropical water plants including water lilies, papyrus, hanging gourds, and the lotus.

In that dusk land of mystic dream
Where dark Osiris sprung,
It bloomed beside his sacred stream,
While yet the world was young;
And every secret Nature told,
Of golden wisdom's power,
Is nestled still in every fold,
Within the Lotos Flower.

—WILLIAM WINTER
"A Lotos Flower," *Wanderers: Being a Collection
of the Poems of William Winter*, 1889

VICTORIA AMAZONICA

One of the main attractions in the Waterlily House at Kew Gardens is its collection of giant Bolivian water lilies, named *Victoria amazonica* (once known as *Victoria regia*) in honor of Queen Victoria. These lilies dwarf every other variety of water lily or lotus and have pads that can grow close to ten feet in diameter. They were so large that Victorians often confidently posed babies and young children on them for photographs.

The lotus and water lily resemble each other strongly. To tell them apart, compare the leaf and flower height. A lotus is typically larger than a water lily. Its leaves and flowers will grow to tower between three and six feet above the water, while a water lily's leaves and flowers often float on the surface.

MAGNOLIA

Magnolia grandiflora

Perseverance

• ◇ • ◇ • ◇ • ◇ •

ne of the most admired of blooming trees in the Victorian garden was the magnolia, particularly the southern magnolia (*Magnolia grandiflora*). In its July 1889 issue, *The Gardener's Chronicle* noted that tree was "the handsomest of the Magnolias with precocious flowers, and the finest of the genus." Sadly, the tree was notoriously difficult to manage in England and, therefore, not as commonly found in gardens. There were other greatly admired varieties of magnolia, though, from China and Japan. China's *Magnolia conspicua*, known as the lily tree or Yulan magnolia, particularly inspired the same journalist to write, "no one ever sees a good plant of *Magnolia conspicua* in full bloom without being filled with admiration, and with the desire to possess such a wonderful object." However, as with the *Magnolia grandiflora*, these trees also seemed to do poorly in the English climate for most amateur gardeners.

Although this species was admired by the Victorians for its beauty and used in gardens to trim walls and arches (whenever they could get it to grow), it was cultivated more often in Victorian American gardens, particularly in the southern United States, from North Carolina south to Florida and west to Texas, where they are native to moist wooded areas with well-drained soil. According to *Flora's Dictionary*, *Magnolia grandiflora* was prized for its elegant, magnificent flowers and its delicious fragrance, "like the flavor of

cold lemonade" and petals that have "the aspect of delicate white leather." In Henry Phillips's *Floral Emblems*, he categorizes *Magnolia grandiflora* as a symbol of dignity, and writes, "The grandeur of this flower is appropriate to the elevated station which it takes in the vegetable kingdom, for in its native soil it advances itself above the forest trees, displaying its dignity, and dispensing its fragrance throughout the woods of Florida." Elizabeth Washington Wirt does not specify why the flower represents perseverance, but the difficulty in cultivating magnolias in England may have contributed to this connection. In floral arrangements, the large glossy leaves of any magnolia species were considered highly decorative and exotic. In Donita Ferguson's *Fun with Flowers* (1939), she suggests forgoing any type of vessel and laying white chrysanthemums over large magnolia leaves as a modern table arrangement.

The first species brought to Europe and cultivated by Bishop Henry Compton in 1688 at the gardens of Fulham Palace in London was the *Magnolia virginiana*, also known as sweetbay, or laurel magnolia. Reverend John Banister, an avid botanist, who had been sent to Virginia by Compton as a missionary to gather and send seeds and cuttings to Fulham, shipped the tree home. Named in honor of the seventeenth-century French botanist Pierre Magnol, the magnolia is an ancient genus of flower of the Magnoliaceae family, that was originally pollinated by beetles and is believed to have appeared before the existence of bees. The plant is native to North, South, and Central America, as well as the Himalayas, and East and South Asia.

Henry Folkard's *Plant Lore, Legends, and Lyrics* says that in India, the blossoms were considered so overwhelmingly fragrant that no Indians would sleep beneath a magnolia tree, or even place a single blossom in a bedroom for fear of death by the power of its perfume. George Piesse writes in *The Art of Perfumery* (1857), that while the scent of the magnolia is "superb," they "are of little use to the perfume manufacturer, the large size of the blossoms and their comparative scarcity prevents their being used." He says an excellent imitation was often made and used by the perfumers of London and Paris. For this he gives a recipe consisting of the pomatums (an infusion of the flower scent with fats or oils) of orange flower, rose, tuberose, and violet with essential citron oil and essential almond oil. He also notes that neroli, or orange flower, when made into a pomatum, can be easily modified to mimic the scent of a sweet pea or a magnolia. In modern perfumery, magnolia is described as a creamy scent with citrus undertones.

There verdure fades never; immortal in bloom,
Soft waves the magnolia its groves of perfume;
And low bends the branch with rich fruitage depress'd,
All glowing like gems in the crowns of the east;
There the bright eye of Nature, in mild glory hovers:
'Tis the land of the sunbeam, —the green isle of lovers!

—REVEREND JAMES WALLIS EASTBURN AND ROBERT C. SANDS
  "Yamoyden," 1817–1820

A STEEL MAGNOLIA

There are two frequently told origins of the arrival of magnolias in France. The first is in the Scottish landscape architect and gardener John Claudius Loudon's 1838 book, *Arboretum et Fruticetum Britannicum*. In his book, Loudon shares the story as told by the French botanist Gabriel Éléonore Merlet de la Boulaye in the new edition of *Du Hamel* (1811–1816), a French treaty on trees and shrubs. Merlet de la Boulaye relates that in 1732, an unknown French naval officer brought a specimen of *Magnolia grandiflora* from the banks of the Mississippi river to his home in La Maillardière, France, a town about five miles outside of Nantes. There, he planted the tree close to his home. Despite the poor soil, the tree managed to flourish. Within only a few years of planting it, the naval officer died. He left his property to his heirs, who mistook the tree for a cherry laurel and took little notice—or care—of it.

In 1758, a professor of botany in Nantes, François Bonamy, happened upon the tree when it was in full bloom and immediately recognized it. Bonamy kept a sample of the tree and, in September 1760, at the meeting of the states of *Bretagne* (Brittany), presented "a fine branch of this magnolia in flower" to Princess de Rohan-Chabot. He shared with all that the tree had reached a height of thirty-five to forty feet and that it was covered in "fine flowers of delicious perfume" every year.

The tree "became a subject of conversation and interest to all there assembled." Word of its magnificence made its way to the court of Louis XV. The king had at one time possessed several small magnolia trees in his

garden at Petit Trianon, but they didn't grow. He wished to possess this magnolia tree that was so well adapted to the French soil. He sent two of his gardeners to La Maillardière to ascertain if it would be possible to transport the magnolia to Versailles without causing injury to the plant, but they determined it would not survive the journey and let it be.

During the war of La Vendée, the tree was damaged and lost most of its branches; later, a nearby home caught fire, damaging the tree's "fine head." At that point, all of the tree's branches were cut off, leaving only the trunk. The tree quickly produced young new shoots, but these were destroyed by a frost. Miraculously, the tree recovered yet again, managing to reach a height of twenty-eight feet and producing between 350 to 400 "elegant and sweet-scented flowers" each year. Loudon wrote that as of 1838, at more than one hundred years old, the tree stood at thirty feet and was still flourishing in the same spot in La Maillardière.

In a second origin story, the magnolia sample was brought to France from Mississippi in 1711 by Lord René Darquistade, a French negotiator who was passionate about botany. He planted this magnolia in the greenhouse at his castle in La Maillardière. For twenty years it never bloomed; one day his wife decided to plant the tree into the ground. After that, it produced large fragrant blooms every year. During the French Revolution, the tree was badly damaged by bullets, fires, and crumbling castle walls. Nonetheless, it managed to survive another fifty years, until 1849.

MARIGOLD

Calendula officinalis and *Tagetes*

Grief

• ◊ • ◊ • ◊ • ◊ •

riginally called "Mary's gold," the marigold was named for the Virgin Mary, which derives from the fact that early Christians placed flowers instead of coins on Mary's altar as an offering. This flower is often used in festivities honoring Mary.

During the Victorian era it was common to give a cordial made from marigolds to those suffering from despair; it was believed to help ease heart palpitations and generally raise the spirit. Some Victorians also believed that presenting a marigold to someone by placing it on their head or heart could convey troubled spirits, troubled love, or weariness within the bestower. Long before the Victorians, the Aztecs were familiar with marigold's ability to calm the nerves and referred to the flower as "the fog." The Romans used marigold for a variety of tasks, including treating warts and dying fabric. They added marigold to cosmetics to help soothe skin and to food for extra flavor. In John Gerarde's *The herball, or, Generall historie of plantes*, he writes that the yellow leaves are dried and stored during the winter throughout Holland, with most grocers and spice merchants keeping them on hand because "no broths are well made without dried marigolds." Marigold was and continues to be referred to as "poor man's saffron" for the color it adds to food and for having a slightly similar taste. *A niewe Herball* prescribes a "distilled water of marygolds" to help with redness or inflammation of the eyes as well as to help purify the air and ward off plague. In the 1816 edition of the English botanist and physician Nicholas Culpeper's *The Complete Herbal* (1653), the editor writes that saffron is "excellent in epidemical diseases, as pestilence, smallpox, and measles," noting that marigolds are "a little less effectual in the smallpox and measles than saffron." Methods he suggests for applying the herb are to mix the leaves with vinegar and bathe in it, or to add fresh or dried flowers to drinks and broths. An interesting skin-mask recipe he offers is "a plaister made with the dry flowers in powder, hog's-grease, turpentine, and rosin [resin], applied to the breast, strengthens and succours [assists] the heart infinitely in fevers, whether pestilential or not."

Sometimes referred to by its genus name, *Calendula*, the marigold is considered an herbaceous plant of the Old World. A common and easy-to-grow flower that comes in vibrant shades of red, orange, and yellow, it is of the Asteraceae, or daisy family. Although this family is known to have a wide native distribution throughout South and Central America as well as parts of Asia and Europe, the exact origin of the common marigold has been difficult to pin down due to a long history of cultivation and how easily it became naturalized around the world. The *Tagetes* marigold genus was also sometimes included in Victorian floriography under the same symbol as calendula. This variety is native to North and South America.

In England, the marigold was used in many divination practices. One, related to telling the fortunes of love, is like the daisy game of "he loves me/ he loves me not." T. F. Dyer describes another method involved combining marigold with a spring of marjoram, thyme, and a little wormwood; drying them out; and turning them into a powder. Afterward, he tells the reader to sift the powder and simmer with "virgin honey, in white vinegar, over a slow fire; with this anoint your stomach, breasts, and lips, lying down, and repeat these words thrice:—'St. Luke, St. Luke, be kind to me, In dream let me my true love see!' This said, hasten to sleep, and in the soft slumbers of night's repose, the very man whom you shall marry shall appear before you."

In Martha Weil's *Magiferous Plants in Medieval English Herbalism*, she mentions the *Middle English Rimed Medical Treatise* (1911), an English translation of a medieval Stockholm manuscript in which marigolds are mentioned as the primary ingredient in a magical amulet to protect against danger and to prevent anyone from speaking ill of the wearer. If the wearer has had property stolen from them, the amulet will produce visions of the thieves while the wearer is asleep, thus revealing their identities. To make this amulet, the manuscript instructs one to gather marigolds during the month of August while the moon is in Virgo and while fasting from food and alcohol so that "out of dedly synn he schuld be clene." The marigolds should then be wrapped in leaves of laurel along with "wolf's tooth," which Weil believes to be wolfsbane. The amulet could be carried in a pocket or worn around the neck.

THE DAY OF THE DEAD

In Mexico, during the multiday celebration of *El Día de los Muertos* (The Day of the Dead) from October 31 to November 2, family members build altars to honor deceased loved ones and to help give them support in their spiritual journeys. Families cover the altars in marigolds, candles, memorabilia, and their loved ones' favorite foods. Traditional foods usually included are *pan de muerto*, a sweet bread that often features a skull or crossbones design on top; artistically decorated sugar skulls; *atole*, a warm and sweet cinnamon-spiced corn-flour porridge; hot chocolate; and *pulque*, a beverage made from fermented agave sap. It's believed that the marigold, also known in Mexico as "the flower of death," helps to guide the spirits to their altars by way of its vibrant colors and strong spicy scent. In Mexico the flower is known as *cempazuchitl*, roughly translated from its Aztec root meaning "twenty petal" or "twenty flowers," which refers to the quantity of petals that make this flower into a fluffy, cheerful ball of color.

In Hilderic Friend's *Flowers and Flower Lore*, he notes that "an old writer" shared the belief that if a marigold didn't open its leaves by seven o'clock in the morning, either rain or thunder would follow later in the day, while Richard Folkard says that Carl Linnaeus stated if the marigold stays open from 9 AM to 3 PM, it foretells a continuance of dry weather. Lastly, Folkard writes that marigolds generally have been considered a good omen between medieval and modern times and that to dream of marigolds is a happy omen "denoting prosperity, riches, success, and a happy and wealthy marriage."

An 1889 issue of *The Gardeners' Chronicle* suggests cutting marigold flowers, tying them into bunches, and hanging them upside down to dry in the same manner as basil, sage, mint, marjoram, or tarragon. Marigolds were recommended as an option to provide charming "patches of bright color" in the garden and were considered an excellent choice for arrangements.

Today, marigolds are commonly gardened around the world and are often paired with edible plants such as chili peppers, tomatoes, or eggplants as a natural method of warding off unwanted insects. They also continue to be added to foods for flavor and coloring. They are sometimes fed to chickens and ducks to make their egg yolks a brighter yellow or bright orange and, in some cases, they can even have a brightening effect on the feet and bills.

Here's flowers for you:
Hot lavender, mints, savory, marjoram:
The marigold, that goes to bed wi' the sun,
And with him rises weeping.

—WILLIAM SHAKESPEARE
The Winter's Tale, act 4, scene 4, line 103, c. 1610–11

MORNING GLORY

Convolvulus

Extinguished hopes or uncertainty

ever opening at night or during wet weather, the morning glory unravels its petals every morning in a curled, parasol-like fashion surrounded by heart-shaped leaves. During the Victorian era, a young woman might have given the flower to a suitor to let him know that she had chosen someone else. Morning glories were quite popular with gardeners because of their hardiness and how little care they require to grow. Additionally, as a fast-growing, climbing plant, it makes an excellent covering for walls and arches. It is also effective in attracting birds, bees, butterflies, and other desirable pollinators.

The morning glory, sometimes called bindweed, is a shrubby flowering vine of the Convolvulaceae family, which also includes sweet potato and water spinach. A popular ornamental plant since the ninth-century Edo period in Japan, this delicate flower comes in a large variety of colors, from blue and yellow to pink-and-white-striped, to a deep, almost black, burgundy.

Its versatility doesn't end there. Three thousand years before Charles Goodyear figured out how to vulcanize rubber, the morning glory was used by Mesoamerican civilizations (in particular the Maya, Aztec, and Olmec peoples) who had discovered that it was useful in converting the latex from the rubber tree and the guayule shrub into rubber because it prevented the latex from drying and turning brittle. Recovered objects made with rubber from these civilizations include sandals, balls, and items of religious or sacrificial purposes. The Aztec priests of Mexico had also discovered that the seeds of morning glory had hallucinogenic properties and would often use them to induce a state of trance in healing rituals and religious ceremonies. Remnants of the seeds have been found in both Aztec and Maya pottery that dates from the Classic period (AD 250–900) to the post-Conquest period (AD 950–1524). Other civilizations of this time that reportedly used morning glory hallucinogens were the Ticitl peoples and the Huichol.

Using hanging baskets to decorate windows was becoming a fashionable trend in the latter Victorian era. Annie Hassard wrote in *Floral Decorations for the Dwelling House* that a basket "never looks well unless it is furnished with some drooping plant round the edge." One of her recommendations for this type of arrangement is to use a dark-green-painted wire basket with blue morning glory and dark-pink Christine geranium.

THE MORNING GLORY AND THE MOON

In India, many plants were named after the moon, including the all-white morning glory known as the half-moon (*Convolvulus turpethum*). This variety is found growing wild in many parts of India and has been a potent source of compounds that are highly antibacterial, anti-inflammatory, analgesic, anti-arthritic, antidiarrheal, and protective against ulcers. Another variety of morning glory called moonflower (*Ipomoea alba*) that's native to tropical and subtropical regions of North and South America, is a night-blooming flower. It's described as having an intoxicating fragrance and being perfect for evening gardens, with its all-white petals that only unfurl at dusk.

NASTURTIUM

Tropaeolum majus

A warlike trophy

• ◇ • ◇ •◦• ◇ •

In ancient Greece and Rome, it was customary for warriors to erect a trophy in the place on the battlefield where they felled an enemy. This usually involved hanging the enemy's bloodied helmet, shield, and armor from a tree branch or pole. The Swedish botanist Carl Linnaeus thought that the leaves of the nasturtium resembled these shields, that the petals were like a golden helmet, and the color, like blood spilled on their armor. He named the flower *Tropaeolum majus* after the Greek word *tropaion*, meaning "trophy."

It was Linnaeus's daughter Elizabeth who observed that the flowers appear to emit a tiny flashing light right at dusk. Now referred to as the Elizabeth Linnaeus phenomenon, we know it is actually an optical illusion created by the way we perceive the color of the nasturtium against the color of twilight.

During the sixteenth century, Spanish botanist Nicolás Monardes brought the nasturtium from Peru to Europe. In his herbal book, *Joyful News out of the Newe Founde Worlde*, he described nasturtiums as "flowers of blood" because of their golden color with red streaks resembling blood on the inner petals. The current name, *nasturtium*, comes from its similarities to watercress, which is called *Nasturtium officinale*, although the two flowers are unrelated to each other. Other names for nasturtium in Old English include *yellow lark's-heels* and *Indian cress*.

Nasturtium seeds were thought to "possess a great power to repel serpents," according to the medieval herbal text, *De viribus herbarum carmen* (1477), attributed to Macer Floridus but possibly written by the Roman poet Aemilius Macer (c. 85–16 BC). It's unclear whether this was a magical idea related to repelling evil or a practical gardening tip for keeping snakes away.

In the 1889 issue of *The Gardeners' Chronicle*, nasturtiums were described as "charming hardy annuals" that are "unrivaled for beauty, effect, and utility." In the standard Victorian garden, nasturtiums were a mainstay as a climbing plant or to add a pop of color on the lining of a flower bed. They were also considered quite the "nose-twister," having a "pungent" scent. Victorians liked to cultivate nasturtiums for their peppery flavor and used the flowers and seeds for pickling or ate them fresh in salads. Nasturtiums continue to be popular in food as well as for adding colorful accents to a bouquet of showier flowers.

The imperial ensign, which, full high advanced,
Shone like a meteor, streaming to the wind.
With gems and golden lustre rich emblazed,
Seraphic arms and trophies.

—JOHN MILTON
Paradise Lost, 1667

BUDDING TALENT

Victorians held juvenile flower shows to share the educational value of participating in flower culture with children. These shows became popular in the 1850s, and some shows, such as one that was held in August 1888 in the London Borough of Southwark, would give pre-grown plants to children early in the year with simple care instructions. The children were to look after the plants, then bring them back a few months later for an examination. If the plant had been attended to properly, the child would win an award, usually a small sum of money.

In other shows, the children were expected to make small arrangements or cultivate plants from seeds. At the Egham Juvenile Floral and Industrial Society's flower show for child gardeners on July 25, 1889, at the Royal Holloway, University of London, there was a junior group for children up to age twelve and a senior group for children up to age seventeen. After submitting a membership fee of three pennies, everyone received six rooted plant cuttings plus six small seed packets mainly comprised of a vibrant purple flower known as dwarf nasturtiums, innocence (*Collinsia bicolor*), candytufts, little darling (also known as mignonette), and a flower known as baby blue eyes (*Nemophila*). The children were encouraged to create floral arrangements in small pots or boxes with the seeds and cuttings given to them. In conclusion to the show, one journalist for *The Gardeners' Chronicle* noted that the exhibition was remarkable "and in most cases the plants were excellent," and observed, "oddly enough, perhaps because of the greater parental care, the plants and seedlings of the juniors were the best."

Some later flower shows also included a "digging and drilling competition for big lads," according to an unnamed journalist for an 1890 issue of *The Gardeners' Chronicle*. The details of the competition aren't given, but the journalist did say that "some capital work was done."

NIGHTSHADE

Solanum nigrum, *Solanum dulcamara*, and *Atropa belladonna*

Truth

• ◇ • ◇ • ◇ • ◇ •

he three most common flowers referred to as "night-shade" are *Solanum nigrum*, known as black nightshade; *Solanum dulcamara*, known as bittersweet nightshade; and *Atropa belladonna*, known as deadly nightshade. All three flowers are in the Solanaceae family and considered toxic. The root of *Solanum* is possibly from the Latin word *solamen*, meaning "solace," however the source for this seems to be untraceable and it's unclear why this was assigned. The plants are known for having many medicinal properties including treatment for skin and digestive disorders, jaundice, and even cancer. These plants were originally native to Eurasia but can be found growing worldwide in a large range of habitats.

The leaves of the bittersweet nightshade are known to taste bitter with a sweet aftertaste when eaten, while the leaves of the deadly nightshade are powerfully narcotic and have been used as a hallucinogen and poison since the time of the ancient Greeks. It's thought that the name *Atropa* was derived from *Atropos*, one of the three Greek goddesses of birth, life, and death. She is the fate that cuts the thread of life with her "abhorred shears" and determines the final destiny of man. The name *belladonna* comes from the Italian, translating to "beautiful lady" and a reference to the practice of women using a diluted eye-drop solution of belladonna to enlarge their pupils for cosmetic purposes during the Renaissance period. Victorian women practiced this little trick, too. It has also been said that they liked to put a little of the pollen from its flower into their tea, as it had hallucinatory effects. Because of their medicinal and poisonous uses, nightshades have been associated with magic and witchcraft throughout history. In Margaret Murray's influential book about the history of witchcraft, *The Witch Cult in Western Europe*, she writes that witches not only had very credible knowledge in the professional art of poisoning, but also that they used belladonna in "flying ointment" recipes and to bandage cuts. The effects of belladonna seeping into their skin produced delirium, excitement, and possibly the impression of flying.

In *Floral Emblems*, Henry Phillips aligns the nightshade with truth. As an example, he points out that receiving news of a social situation can be bitter-sweet, combining elements of happiness with sadness or regret, such as a called-off engagement. He elaborates by saying that however nice or sweet it might be to receive the truth, "it is frequently found a bitter draught to those to whom it is presented."

According to Beverly Seaton's book, *The Language of Flowers*, Victorians often cultivated plants for their sentimental value just as much as for their ornamentation—especially wherever connections to folklore or literature were concerned. In the case of the nightshade plants, Victorians most likely grew them for both their appearance and connections to myth and magic. The mandrake, another member of the Solanaceae family, has its own histor-ical connections to medicine, superstition, and folklore. Like nightshades, it is known to be a powerful hallucinogen and narcotic. Its roots were also said to resemble human forms and it was believed that, if pulled from the ground, they would emit a piercing shriek that could kill anyone who heard it.

Poison, I See, Hath Been His Timeless End

In Shakespeare's *Romeo and Juliet*, *Hamlet*, and *Macbeth*, poison has a part to play. In *Romeo and Juliet*, Juliet ingests a potion that slows her heart rate and places her into a deep sleep, making *Atropa belladonna* the likeliest candidate, as it can be taken in very small quantities and induce these types of effects without causing death. After going to see his dead Juliet in the tomb, Romeo obtains poison from the apothecary to commit suicide, but it's more likely to have been medieval monkshood or potassium cyanide, as his death was immediate. Both cause rapid heart failure.

In *Hamlet*, Prince Hamlet is visited by his father, who tells him how he was murdered:

> *Upon my secure hour thy uncle stole;*
> *With juice of cursed hebenon in a vial;*
> *And in the porches of my ears did pour.*

What "cursed hebenon" is exactly has been a point of speculation ever since. The herb henbane seems like the most obvious choice based on spelling, however other plants that would have been common in the gardens of Shakespeare's time and used for this purpose included hemlock, nightshade, yew, and ebony, each of which possesses its own unique and highly toxic qualities—and all of which would be more harmful than henbane.

Finally, in *Macbeth*, Banquo says:

> *Were such things here as we do speak about?*
> *Or have we eaten on the insane root*
> *That takes the reason prisoner?*

Scholars have also pondered what plant he is referring to as "the insane root." Hemlock, henbane, and deadly nightshade have been suggested as possibilities.

OLEANDER

Nerium oleander

Beware!

• ◇ • ◇ •◇• ◇ •

xtremely showy and fragrant, the oleander was a perfect addition to any Victorian garden. In *Flora's Dictionary*, Elizabeth Washington Wirt warned that, because of its high toxicity, ladies would do well to "*beware* applying it to their lips, as is too generally their custom with their bouquets."

The oleander is a small evergreen tree of the Apocynaceae, or dogbane, family that's native to the Mediterranean region and grows naturally along rivers and streams. The word *oleander* comes from *olea*, the Latin word for olive, because of the resemblance of its leaves to those of an olive tree. Oleander was a popular plant in ancient Roman gardens and is frequently depicted in the flora of murals found in Pompeii.

The banks of the Greek river Meles were sacred to Homer and also thickly set with oleander, which was a plant that was considered to be a bad omen in Italy. In the Roman poet Ovid's (c. 43 BC to AD 17–18) *Epistulae Heroidum*, he wrote a myth, "Hero and Leander," that is sometimes attributed as an origin story for the oleander. Hero was a virgin priestess of Aphrodite who lived in solitude in a tower in the city of Sestos on the banks of the Hellespont Strait. On the opposite bank of the strait was the city Abydos, where Leander lived. After spotting Hero at a festival, Leander fell in love with her and convinced

her to let him swim across the strait to visit her tower every night. Hero agreed to his visits and would light a lantern in her window to help guide his way as he swam. One stormy winter night, a gust of wind extinguished Hero's lantern. With the storm raging outside, she anxiously called out, "Oh, Leander!" as she awaited his safe arrival. Sadly, without the light as a guide, Leander lost his way and was tossed beneath the waves. The next morning, Hero looked out and saw his ravaged body lying on the rocks beneath her tower. In her grief, she flung herself out of the window, hoping to join him in the afterlife. Although the original story ends with their deaths, over time variations came to include a flower clutched in Leander's hand as he lay dead on the beach. Hero removed the flower, which magically continued to grow, thus representing a symbol of everlasting love.

A tradition in Tuscany and Sicily is to cover the dead with oleander blossoms. This is unconnected to the story of Hero and Leander but adds further symbolism to oleander as a somber flower connected with death or bad omens. In many countries such as Russia and India, poisonous or noxious plants such as oleander are considered plants of the devil.

There is a Tuscan legend that ties the oleander to Saint Joseph. The good Joseph possessed an ordinary staff but, when the angel announced to him that he was destined to be the husband of the Virgin Mary, he became so radiant with joy that his staff flowered in his hand. In many paintings depicting Saint Joseph, he is holding a "flowering rod" as a symbol of being divinely chosen. The rod is sometimes shown with small white flowers, too, although it is sometimes portrayed with a colorful bouquet or large white lilies.

Written after Swimming from Sestos to Abydos

Inspired by the myth of Hero and Leander, the Romantic poet Lord Byron swam across the Hellespont Strait on May 3, 1810. He considered this to be his greatest achievement and a few days later, on May 9, wrote "Written after Swimming from Sestos to Abydos":

If, in the month of dark December,
Leander, who was nightly wont
(What maid will not the tale remember?)
To cross thy stream, broad Hellespont!

If, when the wintry tempest roared,
He sped to Hero, nothing loth,
And thus of old thy current poured,
Fair Venus! how I pity both!

For me, degenerate modern wretch,
Though in the genial month of May,
My dripping limbs I faintly stretch,
And think I've done a feat to-day.

But since he crossed the rapid tide,
According to the doubtful story,
To woo,—and—Lord knows what beside,
And swam for Love, as I for Glory;

'Twere hard to say who fared the best:
Sad mortals! thus the Gods still plague you!
He lost his labour, I my jest:
For he was drowned, and I've the ague.

ORCHID

Orchidaceae

BEE ORCHID: Industry
BUTTERFLY ORCHID: Cheerfulness
FLY ORCHID: Error
FROG ORCHID: Disgust
SPIDER ORCHID: Adroitness

• ◇ • ◇ • ◇ • ◇ •

uring the Victorian era, horticulture was a popular pastime, as was collecting natural specimens, which Victorians liked to display en masse in cabinets of curiosity. Although orchids existed in England for quite some time, they were not popular for cultivation until a new South American variety was introduced to London in 1818 by scientist William John Swainson. As with many old stories, the details of how exactly this orchid arrived have been told in various romanticized legends over the years. In one version, Swainson was on an expedition in Brazil to collect lichen and fern specimens and, when unable to find suitable material for packing up his finds to send them to W. Jackson Hooker, Regius Professor at Glasgow, he used what he had on hand: the orchid *Cattleya labiata vera*. The other version of the story, which modern botanists feel is more accurate, is that Swainson had seen this orchid in the wild and knew that William Cattley, an avid horticulturist and one of Swainson's tropical plant collectors, would be interested in having one as well. Swainson packed up the orchid, which may have also been wrapped in ferns to protect it, and sent it to Cattley's hothouse in Barnet, England. Cattley's orchid flowered in London in November 1818. The following year, another one of Swainson's orchids of the same variety, which had been sent to Glasgow, bloomed, too. In 1821, the English botanist John Lindley named the orchid the *Cattleya* after Cattley, and this variety later came to be known as the corsage orchid.

While the plant is available in various colors today, English landscape painter Henry Moon's illustration for orchidologist Frederick Sander's four-volume *Reichenbachia: Orchids Illustrated and Described* depicts Swainson's orchid with rosy pink petals that are lightly ruffled on the edges and a center lip of white and yellow with red streaks. At the time of its introduction, the flower was described as the only orchid capable of having blooms year-round. Sander was the official Royal Orchid Grower to Queen Victoria. Nicknamed the Orchid King, he employed twenty-three orchid hunters who traversed the globe, regularly shipping thousands—and possibly millions—of orchid specimens back to England.

After the discovery of the *Cattleya labiata vera*, orchid collecting quickly became an obsessive offshoot of the horticulture rage, as the flower was viewed as a unique rarity. Orchid hunting and collecting became a hobby for the very wealthy, who cultivated them in their greenhouses and embarked upon expeditions worldwide in search of the rarest species, regardless of the amount of time, money, or danger involved. In fact, orchid hunting and collecting became such an obsession among England's rich, that it was referred to as "orchidelirium," or orchid fever. Orchid fever lasted for decades, tapering off at the end of the nineteenth century, as botanists found ways to reproduce and hybridize the flowers more efficiently. These new hybridized varieties produced beautiful results and had the same care and cultivation requirements of species imported from exotic locations without the risk and expense of traveling to parts unknown to obtain them, or just simply the high cost of buying them. As the plants became more affordable and readily available, orchid fever waned.

Bee orchid
Ophrys apifera

Butterfly orchid
Platanthera bifolia

Fly orchid
Ophrys insectifera

Frog orchid
Coeloglossum viride

Early spider orchid
Ophrys sphegodes

Darwin's orchid
Angraecum sesquipedale

Morgan's sphinx moth
Xanthopan morganii
of the Sphingidae hawk
moth family

According to Victorian writer and orchid fancier Frederick Boyle, orchid fever may have been both a literal and figurative term. In his book, *About orchids; a chat*, he writes, "the honest youth, not very strong perhaps in an English climate, went bravely forth into the unhealthiest parts of unhealthy lands, where food is very scarce, and very, very rough; where he was wet through day after day, for weeks at a time; where 'the fever,' of varied sort, comes as regularly as Sunday." He goes on to say that he "could make out a startling list of the martyrs of orchidology" then follows with a partial list of unfortunate men who died in pursuit of orchids.

Orchids are flowering plants of the Orchidaceae family, which is the second-largest plant family next to the Asteraceae, or daisy, family. They are native to the Mediterranean region and some tropical climates of Asia and South and Central America. The orchid's name is derived from the Greek word *orkibis*, which means "testicle," and refers to its tube-shaped roots. In ancient Greece, orchids were thought to have medicinal properties, to be an aphrodisiac, and to be a method by which to control the sex of an unborn child. It was thought that if the mother ate a large orchid root she would have a boy, and if she ate a smaller root she would have a girl.

In Henry Lyte's *A niewe Herball*, he described five kinds of orchid that grew around England; they are variously referred to as "orchis," "satyrion," "serapias," "standergrasse," or "standelwurte." He wrote that the roots of the orchid were edible and full of a sap, and that, as suggested by the Greeks, when ingested, could incite lust, or as he put it, "provoketh Venus," and strengthen or nourish the body.

Charles Darwin was deeply fascinated by orchids and the evolutionary relationships they had with their insect pollinators. In 1862 he published *Fertilisation of Orchids*, a follow-up to *On the Origin of Species*. In this new book, he gave detailed demonstrations of how orchids had developed advantageous characteristics to attract specific moths and vice versa. Not only did this book demonstrate the power of his evolutionary theory, but it helped to create testable predictions.

Darwin's orchid, for example, is a star-shaped orchid from Madagascar that has an unusual, nearly foot-long nectar tube. In 1862, Darwin predicted that an insect capable of pollinating this flower would have to exist for this flower to survive. He was right, and the pollinator was eventually identified. In 1907, more than forty years after Darwin had made this prediction, the hawk moth was discovered in Madagascar, not far from the original location where Darwin's orchid was found. The hawk moth has a proboscis that can extend between ten and eleven inches, long enough to reach the nectar in the orchid's tube. Darwin discovered that pollination by a single insect occurred in other orchid species as well. The bee orchid only attracts one pollinator, the male *Eucera*, a type of solitary, long-horned bee, while the fly orchid only attracts two species of solitary, black male wasps, the *Argogorytes mystaceus* and the *Scoliidae*. Both orchids do so by emitting a scent that mimics the female pheromones of the specific insect.

Henry Phillips's *Floral Emblems* says that the bee, butterfly, fly, frog, and spider orchids were thought to closely resemble the insect or animal that they're named after and that each symbolizes a quality typically associated with its respective creature. The bee orchid, for example, has a fuzzy center lobe that is brown with yellow spots and stripes. Since bees are hard workers, the flower came to represent industry. The butterfly orchid was thought to have an airy, showy quality that connotes cheerfulness. The frog orchid has a modified irregular petal in its center that comes down like a tongue, while the spider orchid has a very large center petal that's somewhat round and brown. The fly orchid has the appearance of black flies, in place of flowers, resting on the stem, which comes off as an error of nature. Despite its resemblance to a bee, the bee orchid has the advantage of being the only European orchid not reliant on insects for pollination. There are more than twenty thousand known species of orchid and although *Phalaenopsis*, or moth orchids, were considered more beautiful, it was primarily for their resemblance to other elements of nature that these five particular orchids were chosen to be included in the language of flowers lists over other more exotic species.

THE REAL VANILLA
IS NOT SO VANILLA

Vanilla's synonymity with the generic, boring, or bland may have roots in the fact that it is used pervasively in processed, low-fat, and low-carb products to make them tastier, including soda, liquor, baked goods, ice cream, sorbet, and frozen yogurt. It's also used in other processed commercial foods, too. Unfortunately, the real reason vanilla is maligned is that, very often, we are not tasting vanilla at all, but vanillin, a synthetic form of vanilla that is in the plant in small amounts and manufactured for use in processed foods. It lacks the subtle taste and aroma of the real thing. It is also much cheaper to make.

Vanilla's taste and aroma is complex. More than 250 different flavor and aroma components have been detected in vanilla extract and, for centuries, the bean was considered exotic, a culinary luxury among the European elite. According to Patricia Rain's book *Vanilla: The Cultural History of the World's Favorite Flavor and Fragrance,* Thomas Jefferson, after enjoying vanilla-flavored sweets in France, imported the vanilla bean to America in the late eighteenth century and used it to flavor ice cream. Jefferson may have enjoyed it, but Rain posits that the taste may have seemed unremarkable to Americans, who were used to ice cream flavored with stronger tastes, such as fruit or nuts. She also says that its flavor is often used today as the basis for another flavor, not for vanilla itself.

The vanilla bean, the source of real vanilla extract and flavoring, is the product of the world's only fruit-producing orchid, *Vanilla planifolia.* Indigenous to Mexico and pollinated by the indigenous and endangered *Melipona* bee, it's a fussy flower, requiring a tropical environment, steady rainfall, and the right balance of sun and shade. Growing, harvesting, and curing vanilla is a labor-intensive process that can take up to five years. Every stage of cultivating the vanilla bean must be done by hand, beginning with pollinating its pale yellow, odorless flower. This must be done within a few hours on a single day in the plant's harvesting cycle, as this is the only time it blooms. If not pollinated in this short window, the flower dies.

The vanilla bean is now cultivated worldwide. Today, Madagascar produces about 80 percent of the world's vanilla, followed by China and Mexico.

Although orchid fever eventually faded, at least from the broader public consciousness, orchid shows, conferences, and national collectives of orchid enthusiasts ranging from amateur gardeners to professional horticulturists remain active today. One well-known American horticulturist and rare plant dealer, John Laroche, had a lifelong passion for orchids and an eventual obsession with the wild ghost orchid. He believed that if he could obtain and clone this species, he would be able turn a large profit. In the early 1990s, while working with the Seminole tribe of south Florida on the Fakahatchee Strand State Preserve, he was arrested for poaching the rare flower from its swamps. Susan Orlean investigated Laroche's story for *The New Yorker* in her 1995 article "The Orchid Thief." The story was eventually published as a book of the same title, and later adapted into the popular 2002 movie, *Adaptation*, directed by Spike Jonze and starring Meryl Streep, Chris Cooper, and Nicolas Cage.

◊ • ◊ • ◊ • ◊ •

It is mere virtue which makes me
not wish to examine more orchids;
for I like it far better than writing about
varieties of cocks & Hens & Ducks.

—CHARLES DARWIN
to Joseph Dalton Hooker, 1861

CONSOLATION ARISING FROM THOUGHTS

Pansy vase with snowdrops inspired by an illustration from
Henry Phillips's *Floral Emblems* (1825)

PANSY

Viola tricolor

You occupy my thoughts

• ◇ • ◇ • ◇ • ◇ •

The wild pansy as a symbol for thoughts of love can be traced back to Shakespeare's plays *A Midsummer Night's Dream*, *Hamlet*, and *The Taming of the Shrew*. In *A Midsummer Night's Dream* (act 2, scene 1), the fairy king Oberon recounts:

> *Cupid all arm'd: a certain aim he took*
> *At a fair vestal, throned by the west,*
> *And loos'd his love-shaft smartly from his bow,*
> *As it should pierce a hundred thousand hearts.*
> ....
> *Yet mark'd I where the bolt of Cupid fell:*
> *It fell upon a little western flower,—*
> *Before milk-white, now purple with love's wound,—*
> *And maidens call it love-in-idleness.*
> *Fetch me that flower: the herb I shew'd thee once;*
> *The juice of it on sleeping eye-lids laid,*
> *Will make or man or woman madly dote*
> *Upon the next live creature that it sees.*

Oberon proceeds to use a love potion made of pansies on his sleeping wife, Titania, to trick her into falling in love with the first creature she sees upon waking. Thereafter, the pansy became commonly referred to as "love-in-idleness" and was used in making love potions or casting spells.

In *Hamlet*, there is a scene where Ophelia, who has been gathering various herbs and flowers while lamenting the death of her father, Polonius, arrives at court. She rambles on about each plant while distributing them among those who are present; she gives rosemary and pansies to her brother, Laertes, telling him they symbolize remembrance and thoughts.

Last, in *The Taming of the Shrew*, upon arriving in the Italian city of Padua, the young student Lucentio spots Baptista Minola walking through a crowd with his daughters, Katherine, the shrew, and her amiable younger sister, Bianca. Lucentio falls in love with Bianca on first sight and tells his manservant Tranio that he never thought it likely that he could feel the effects of "love in idleness" that he's experiencing at that moment.

Pansies are a part of the *Viola* genus, which is the largest genus of flowering plants within the violet (Violaceae) family. Members of the *Viola* genus typically have scalloped or heart-shaped leaves and rounded, multicolored petals. A variety of medicinal uses for the pansy have been recorded through history including treatment for eczema and cancer, and in one Irish herbology from 1735, the ability to cure children of convulsions, inflammation, and fever.

The pansy we enjoy today is a hybridization of an ancient but still common medieval wild pansy, known as heart's ease. Sometime during the fifteenth century the flower was renamed *pansy* from the French adjective *pensée* (pensive) because it resembled a bowed head looking down in deep thought. If a pansy was given in an upright position, the Victorians interpreted the gesture to mean "think of me," but if presented in a downward position, they read the message as "forget me." Other lore suggests that a lover's future can be read by picking one of the upper petals of a tricolor variety and counting the veins that run through it. Four veins mean there's hope; seven, eternal love; eight, fickleness; nine, a change of heart; eleven, an early death. If you dream about the flower, you can expect to have troubles with a good friend.

Until the nineteenth century, most people considered the pansy a weed. But thanks to the Victorians, two people in particular, it became a popular garden flower. The most notable cultivator was Lady Mary Elizabeth Bennet (1785–1861), the daughter of the 4th Earl of Tankerville and Lady Tankerville, née Emma Colebrooke, a well-known collector of exotic plants. Lady Tankerville employed artists to illustrate her specimens, too, and her collection of more than six hundred botanical illustrations still resides at Kew Gardens. In 1788, the nun's orchid (*Phaius tankervillae*) flowered, making it the first tropical orchid to be grown and flowered in England, an event that stimulated interest in the growing of exotic orchids. The flower is one of many plants named for Lady Tankerville.

Lady Mary Elizabeth Bennet shared her mother's intense horticultural interests. With the help of her father's gardener, William Richardson, Lady Bennet crossbred a wide variety of *Viola tricolor* pansies, ultimately expanding the species' color palette while stabilizing the solid colors, enlarging the flowers, and selecting plants to produce more prominent whiskers (the deep lines that radiate from the center). She introduced her flowers to the horticultural world in 1812 to much acclaim, and today, she is considered the mother of the modern pansy.

The story then takes a little twist. A nurseryman, Mr. Lee, was so impressed by Bennet's hybrids that he brought them to another aristocrat experimenting with *Viola tricolor*, Lord Gambier, and his gardener William Thompson, at Iver, Buckinghamshire. Lord Gambier introduced Russian species into the genetic mix. By 1833 there were four hundred named pansies, more or less the same plants we know today.

THE FLOWER WITH A FACE

In William Cuthbertson's *Pansies, Violas, & Violets* (1910), he writes that between 1814 and 1830 florists primarily judged pansies by their color, size, and shape. While attempting to develop new varieties to meet these standards, William Thompson, estate gardener to Lord Gambier at Iver, eventually produced the first pansy that could reliably reproduce a dark-purple blotch on each of its petals. In 1839 Lord Gambier released these specimens to the public under the name *Medora*. These blotches, one on each petal, have come to be known as the face of the flower, a characteristic that endears pansies to gardeners the world over.

• ◊ • ◊ • ◊ • ◊ •

I pray, what flowers are these?
The pansy this,
O, that's for lover's thoughts.

—GEORGE CHAPMAN
All Fools, act 2, scene 1, 1605

PEONY

Paeonia

Anger or bashful shame

• ◇ • ◇ • ◇ • ◇ •

looming in April and into early May, peonies are a sign that we're fully into spring. Their enormous frilly blooms, delicate fragrance, and fairly wide variety of colors have long made peonies a popular flower, despite the fact that the blooms are short-lived—about seven to ten days. A hardy perennial native to Asia, North America, and parts of Europe, these ancient flowering woody shrubs are part of the *Paeonia* genus, the only genus in the Paeoniaceae family with more than 6,500 known cultivars. Some varieties, such as the white-and-raspberry-colored Hélène Martin tree peony or the gold-colored Bartzella Itoh hybrid peony can produce blossoms as wide as eight to ten inches. The plant's roots survive well in cold conditions and are also drought tolerant, making them a simple plant to care for. Maintained properly, some species can live as long as one hundred years, with the first blooms being identical to the last. The peony is truly an heirloom plant.

Both tree and herbaceous peonies were cultivated in ancient China and Japan, with records of the plants being well established across China by AD 536. The first known peony tree, *Paeonia suffruticosa*, was imported to Japan from China in AD 724. One of the most commonly grown peonies, *Paeonia lactiflora*, also known as the Chinese peony or common garden peony, was originally known as *Paeonia albiflora* and originated in Siberia and China. Peonies were also recorded for use in foods and medicine. According to the Institute for Traditional Medicine in Portland, Oregon, peony was allegedly a favorite flavoring of Confucius (551–479 BC), who was said to eat nothing without its sauce.

In Alice Harding's 1907 work, *The Book of the Peony*, she writes that tree peonies were favored over the shrub variety and referred to in China as *sho yo*, meaning "most beautiful" and ranked as China's "king of flowers." In China, peonies were given as a symbol of remembrance after separation. In 1086, Chinese gardeners took more interest in improving upon the peony for ornamental purposes, to increase the variety of size and color, and by 1596 there were thirty known varieties. The Japanese name for peony was *skakuyaku*, which is possibly a corruption of *sho yo*. The Japanese often featured the flower in art and literature, such as this poem by Bashō: "Peony / the bee can't bear / to part."

The name *peony* comes from Paean who, according to Homer, was the designated physician to the Greek gods. This gives the flower's name an ancient connection to the word for healing. The word was sometimes invoked in reference to any God that had the power to heal. In Homer's *Iliad*, Paen healed Ares's battle wound; in the *Odyssey*, after Hades was shot with an arrow by Hercules, Paean saved him, too.

In Pliny the Elder's *Natural History* (c. AD 77–79), he cites Homer's reference to Paean and writes that the peony can be used as a remedy against "illusions caused by the Fauni in sleep. It is generally recommended to take it up at night for if the wood-pecker of Mars should perceive a person doing so, it will immediately attack out the eyes in defense of the plant."

Pliny is referring to an ancient Roman myth in which Picus, a king and the son of the god Saturn, refuses the advances of Circe, the goddess of magic, in favor of his wife, the nymph Canens, the personification of song. In anger, Circe turns him into a woodpecker. In other Roman versions of this

story, Picus was the son of Mars, the god of war. Picus and Canens were the parents of Faunus, known in Greek stories as Pan, the god of wild nature. The fauni were known as woodland nymphs or spirits that caused nightmares and mental illness. In Henry Lyte's *A niewe Herball*, he recommends mixing twelve to fifteen peony seeds with wine or mead to help with nightmares. He also suggests taking dried peony root with meade to help with "tormentes of the belly" and tying dried peony root around one's neck to ward off sickness.

Medieval Europeans believed that peonies could ward off evil and magic. In *The Folklore of Plants*, T. F. Dyer writes that some plants were used in exorcisms for their "reputed antagonism to all Satanic influences," and that some could render the devil powerless. He shares that in "ancient times" the peony was used for this purpose along with black hellebore and mugwort. In Richard Folkard's *Plant Lore, Legends, and Lyrics*, he writes that "peony drives away tempests and dispels enchantments." He also shares a story of the peony's significance in the language of flowers in a poem by René Rapin (1621–1687):

> *Erect in all her crimson pomp you'll see*
> *With bushy leaves the graceful Piony,*
> *Whose blushes might the praise of virtue claim,*
> *But her vile scent betrays they rise from shame.*
> *Happy her form, and innocent her red,*
> *If, while Alcinous' bleating flock she fed,*
> *An heavenly lover had not sought her bed;*
> *'Twas Phœbus' crime, who to his arms allured*
> *A maid from all mankind by pride secured.*

Here, the shepherdess Alcinous makes love with the sun god, Phoebus (a Greek and Roman epithet for Apollo), and, upon the realization that the nymph Piony has seen them, they rise in shame. Later, *Floral Emblems* assigned the meaning "bashful shame" to the peony. *Flora's Dictionary* pairs the peony with "anger" but doesn't explain why.

The English have had a fondness for the peony since medieval times. Monk and gardening writer Alexander Neckam wrote in his book *De Naturis Rerum* (c. 1190) that a "noble garden" should "be adorned with roses and lilies, turnsole, violets and mandrake; there you should have…fennel, coriander…and peonies." He's referring to *Paeonia officinalis*, the common garden peony. Native to southern Europe, from France to Albania, this is the peony referred to in Greek and Roman mythology. During the Tudor period (1485–1603), peonies were often written about in conjunction with other garden favorites such as rose, jasmine, lilies, and lavender. The English had a variety of nicknames for the flower, too, including "hundred-bladed rose" and "rose royale."

Peonies have been valuable in landscape architecture for protecting other plants around them and for making borders along walkways or walls because they're large and highly ornamental. The first tree peony to be planted in England was secured by Sir Joseph Banks and brought to Kew Gardens from China by the East India Company in 1787. This specimen failed to thrive and a replacement batch of peonies was shipped in 1794. Many of these peonies died on the voyage, but three survived, including Rosea, a variety with deep pink flowers. These survivors were successfully grown and propagated at Kew, then distributed to other British gardens. As of 1838 there were a dozen known varieties of peony in England, with many of them imported from French growers. It's not clear when tree peonies were introduced to the United States, but it's thought that they were imported from Europe around 1820.

Victorians loved the peony's large, showy blooms, which made the flower a popular choice to exhibit at flower shows, but there is little information about their use for indoor arrangements—perhaps showing them at home would be considered immodest. In her 1947 book, *Flower Arrangements for Everyone*, Dorothy Biddle notes that single Japanese types of peonies were better suited to indoor arrangement than the larger double blooms, and that larger blooms should be arranged with large magnolia leaves. In a modern bouquet depicted in a spring 2018 issue of *Southern Living*, cut peony buds that aren't yet open are immediately placed in water. This way the full blooming process can be enjoyed. Additionally, peonies can be used as decoration in anything from wedding bouquets, party garlands, living-room accents, or even as a lush, fluffy topper for cakes.

• ◊ • ◊ • ◊ • ◊ •

Whatever is begun in anger ends in shame.

—BENJAMIN FRANKLIN
Poor Richard's Almanack, 1733

A RAINBOW OF PEONIES

Through extensive hybridization, peonies are capable of naturally growing in every shade of color except for a true blue (although some come close with lilac or lavender). Striking colors can be seen in the Sappho variety, which takes a vivid, almost-neon purple, and the Captain's Concubine, which produces frilly white-edged petals resembling butterfly wings that turn a dark pink as they approach the heart of the blossom. Another variety known as Gauguin is meant to be reminiscent of the famous painter's palette and produces dusty yellow-pink petals that have a dark-pink netted pattern over them. Alternatively, varieties such as the Chinese Dragon produce solid crimson flowers with lacy, bronze-tinted foliage swirling behind the blossoms, suggesting the scales of a dragon in movement. There are also varieties of black tree peony such as the Black Panther or Black Pirate, which produce a burgundy so deep that the flower is almost black.

PERIWINKLE

Vinca

Pleasures of memory

• ◇ • ◇ • ◇ • ◇ •

The periwinkle as an emblem of the "pleasures of memory" is believed to have originated from a passage in philosopher Jean-Jacques Rousseau's 1782 autobiography, *Confessions*. Sometime in the 1730s, when visiting his mistress and mentor Françoise-Louise de Warens's house at Charmettes, near Chambèry, France, the two ventured out, whereupon Rousseau saw a periwinkle for the first time. He writes: "Of these recollections I shall relate one example, which may give some idea of their force and precision....As we passed along, she saw something blue in the hedge, and said, 'There's some periwinkle in flower yet!' I had never seen any before, nor did I stop to examine this: my sight is too short to distinguish plants on the ground, and I only cast a look at this as I passed: an interval of near thirty years had elapsed before I saw any more periwinkle, at least before I observed it, when being at Cressier in 1764, with my friend, M. du Peyrou, we went up a small mountain...walking and looking among the bushes, I exclaimed with rapture, 'Ah, there's some periwinkle!' The reader may judge by this impression, made by so small an incident, what an effect must have been produced by every occurrence of that time."

A small, wild, flowering shrub with star-shaped flowers that grow in light blue, purple-blue, and white, the periwinkle belongs to the Apocynaceae

(dogbane) family, which is native to Europe and some parts of Asia and Africa. The periwinkle is often referred to by its genus, *Vinca*, which comes from the Latin word *pervincire*, meaning "to bind" or "to entwine." The color periwinkle is named after the flower.

During the Victorian era, periwinkles were "found in every garden" and the Madagascar periwinkle was "a popular green-house plant, flowering the greater part of the year," according to *Flora's Dictionary*. In Annie Hassard's *Floral Decorations for the Dwelling House*, she writes that "groups of plants arranged with good effect in sitting-rooms, or on staircases, are important objects, and should, therefore, be grouped with care and taste." In her long list of acceptable flowers, she recommends the dwarf periwinkle (*Vinca minor*) as one such tasteful option to be included in one of these arrangements. In *The Book of Cut Flowers*, R. P. Brotherston wrote that periwinkle drooping over the edge of a vase made a "desirable setting to other flowers," confirming the flower's popularity at the time.

Per Henry Lyte's *A niewe Herball*, the flower's medicinal uses once included alleviating dysentery and its associated pains by drinking wine, milk, or rose oil, with periwinkle mixed in. Other remedies included chewing periwinkle for toothaches, applying the chewed paste to help with "stinging from venomous beasts," and plugging the nose with the flowers to stop a nosebleed. In modern medicine, extracts from the Madagascar periwinkle, a relative of the common periwinkle that is no longer placed in the *Vinca* genus, have been shown to be useful for a variety of ailments from sore throats to cancer treatments.

Because periwinkles grow quickly and require little care, they are popular as an ornamental ground cover in gardens and were once the traditional choice for ground cover in cemeteries. According to T. F. Dyer's *The Folklore of Plants*, the ancient Greeks and Romans placed special emphasis on flowers to be laid across graves. The Romans valued roses as a funeral flower and would often leave special instructions for these to be planted on their graves. Following in this tradition, in the "modern times" of 1889, Dyer wrote that periwinkle had come to be nicknamed "death's flower" as it was commonly

PERIWINKLE LOVE POTIONS

It was common during the Middle Ages to falsely attribute works to well-known figures for the purposes of gaining attention and credibility. As an example, *The Book of Secrets of Albertus Magnus* is an anonymously written collection of magical texts by followers of the bishop Albertus Magnus (1200–1280), an influential German friar, bishop, theologian, and philosopher. After his death, he was canonized as a Catholic saint and became known as Saint Albert the Great. First printed in 1650, the book contains numerous spells and potions for daily life. Not only was it one of the more popular, widely circulated, and reprinted texts of the time, but it also has helped paint a portrait of medieval magical culture and medicine for modern historians—even though no serious scholars or medical practitioners at the time contributed to these texts or seemed to pay much attention to them.

One recipe in this book includes wrapping periwinkle with earthworms, then beating it into a powder. The powder was then to be combined with houseleek and added to meat. Once consumed by husband and wife, the mixture would induce love between them. In the 1816 edition of Nicholas Culpeper's *The Complete Herbal* (1653), the editor concurs: "when the leaves of periwinkle are chewed by a husband and wife at the same time, this will create love between them." He also suggests that periwinkle is a "good female medicine, and may be used with advantage in hysteric and other fits" as well as aiding with nervous disorders and nightmares.

used in Italy, in Tuscany in particular, to adorn children's graves. In Germany the pink Madagascar periwinkle was used for the same purpose.

In the United States, periwinkle was placed so commonly on the unmarked graves of black slaves that looking for periwinkle patches has become a useful method in locating many of these lost burial grounds. This fact also contributed to the development of the National Burial Database of Enslaved Americans and The Periwinkle Initiative, organizations dedicated to the memory and preservation of the history of those enslaved in America.

CHINA PINK

Dianthus chinensis

Aversion

• ◊ • ◊ • ◊ • ◊ •

inks, a flowering herbaceous plant of the *Dianthus* genus, were popular in Victorian gardens for their variety of colors and delicate lacy flowers. *The Book of Cut Flowers* notes that pinks are "cherished by many for bunching like violets, or like primroses." The China pink was preferable over other varieties of pinks for its lack of scent and "the most beautiful" marks of coloring, according to *Flora's Dictionary*. The book also mentions mountain pinks and red pinks but with less enthusiasm. All of this points to why, over more common varieties, the China pink was more often included in various books about the language of flowers. The center of the flower is sometimes thought to resemble an eye, and the Dutch term *pinck oogen* meaning "small or half-closed eyes," may be the origin of the name *pink*. It's also thought the English word for the color pink may have also come from the flower.

The China pink is native to China, Korea, Mongolia, and Russia. It grows well on mountainsides and dry, sandy areas. Although carnations and pinks have been cultivated in Europe and England for many centuries, information on how the specific China pink cultivar arrived in England is sparse. In *Floral Emblems*, Henry Phillips writes that the symbolism for the China pink may have come from China's earlier isolationist policies and their "aversion"

to interacting with other countries. Pinks once had the nickname "sops-in-wine," most likely because, like the carnation, some varieties were occasionally added to wine as an inexpensive alternative to Indian clove. Elizabeth Washington Wirt gives this nickname solely to the carnation.

SINK THE PINK

In Scotland some old folk stories and games that have been passed down through the generations through stories or songs are variations of ancient war songs or battle cries that continued be modified over the years, while the origins of others aren't entirely known. One such example of the latter is the game Three Flowers. To play, two boys would leave a larger group of boys and girls to designate whether each of those remaining were either a rose, a pink, or a gillyflower. The two would return to the group, whereupon they'd sing this rhyme to a girl of their choosing:

> My mistress sent me unto thine,
> Wi' three young flowers baith fair and fine:—
> The pink, the rose, and the gillyflower,
> And as they here do stand,
> Whilk will ye sink, whilk will ye swim,
> And whilk bring hame to land?

This girl would then have to guess the chosen pairings, name each flower, and say, "I will sink the pink, swim the rose, and bring hame the gillyflower to land." Afterward, the two children would reveal the original pairings. Amusement comes with error: by choosing incorrectly, the girl may slight her best friend or the boy she likes most; by choosing correctly, she may, on the other hand, align herself with someone she doesn't like at all. Either way, the results were thought to be a great source of entertainment.

POPPY

Papaver rhoeas
RED: Consolation to the sick

Papaver somniferum
WHITE: Sleep of the heart

• ◊ • ◊ • ◊ • ◊ •

ccording to T. F. Dyer's *The Folklore of Plants*, poppies were employed in the art of "love-divination" with their "prophetic leaves," and also possessed "some magical effect upon the fortunes of lovers" during the Middle Ages. In fact, a man would carry the blossoms in his pocket with the "success in love being indicated in proportion as they lost or retained their freshness." Another poppy he mentions, which isn't often discussed in other records, is the horned, or sea poppy. In Folkard's *Plant Lore, Legends, and Lyrics*, he writes that witches and sorcerers used the horned poppy in various spells and incantations. He shares this excerpt from a book of witches' songs:

> *Yes, I have brought to help our vows,*
> *Horned Poppy, Cypress-boughs,*
> *The Fig-tree wild that grows on tombs,*
> *And juice that from the Larch-tree comes.*

During the Victorian era, poppies had been so diversified through propagation that, according to Elizabeth Washington Wirt's *Flora's Dictionary*, "two plants [were] seldom alike in their flowers." Wirt also notes that in the sixteenth century, couples would use poppy petals to prove the sincerity of their love.

They would place a poppy petal in the hollow of the palm of their left hand, then strike it with their right. If a snapping sound was heard, this denoted true attachment; if not, faithlessness. The poppy is one of the many flowers considered sacred to Aphrodite, the Greek goddess of love, and has been seen in hieroglyphs describing her, adding a further link to its connection with love.

In Victorian gardening, poppies were described as beautiful but often inconsistent in form. In particular the Shirley poppy, created by the Reverend William Wilkes in 1880, is derived from the wild European field poppy and described in an 1889 issue of *The Gardeners' Chronicle* as "wondrously beautiful" and having "shades of indescribable hues, so exquisitely refined and pleasing that even a blasé florist like myself can get into a state of enthusiasm over them." The writer also expresses chagrin over the fact that this poppy has so many qualities in common with other "evolved garden flowers" but why this poppy does "not adhere to form [they] cannot comprehend, as the process of selection has been the work of years." This variety can grow in a range of colors and has semi-double and double blossoms. There are many newer cultivars of the Shirley poppy, including mother of pearl, which can produce misty gray or mauve flowers in addition to pinks, lilacs, and whites, and Pandora, which can produce rich burgundy flowers with silvery stripes.

The poppy is a member of the Papaveraceae family, which is in the Ranunculales order, making poppies a sister family of Ranunculaceae (buttercups and water crowfoots). Although the poppy family includes a few varieties, the two that are most commonly grown for commercial purposes are the opium poppy, *Papaver somniferum*, and the red field poppy, *Papaver rhoeas*. A third variety native to California and not as common worldwide is the golden poppy, *Eschscholzia californica*. Although poppies have naturally been found in Asia and Europe for many centuries, the oldest fossil records of the poppy family are from the Mediterranean area with seeds of the opium poppy that date from the early Neolithic era. This evidence has also shown that humans have been using opium poppies as a source of food and medicine, as well as an ingredient in psychoactive beverages since that time.

POPPY NOTES

The Roman goddess of agriculture, Ceres, is often depicted holding poppies and wheat in her outstretched hands, possibly because wild poppies are sometimes found growing in wheat fields. When Ceres's daughter Proserpina is abducted by Juno, god of the underworld, the Roman myth relayed that he gave Ceres poppies to assuage her grief.

• ◊ •

In Ovid's poem "Fasti," he describes the goddess of night, Nyx, as a primordial deity crowned in poppies: "Her calm brow wreathed with poppies night drew on and in her brain brought darkling dreams."

• ◊ •

After World War I, wild red poppies sprang up in the trenches and grounds at Flanders Fields in France, an area encompassing the East and West Flanders regions of Belgium as well as parts of the area known as French Flanders, where many soldiers had perished during battle. The poppy has since become the symbol of Remembrance Day, observed on November 11 by the Commonwealth of Nations, in honor of the sacrifice these soldiers made.

Opium, morphine, and heroin, derived from the seeds of the opium poppy, have been used as a recreational, medicinal, and ceremonial drug for centuries. In Henry Lyte's *A niewe Herball*, he describes numerous uses for the plant, from making a syrup to help with sleep, indigestion, or coughing, by boiling the poppy's leaves, seeds, or flower heads in water or wine, to making dried poppy heads into a topical paste with rose or sweet almond oil, myrrh, and saffron for headaches or earaches. He also offers a recipe for a topical paste for "hoate tumors, which have need of cooling" as well as a more liquid remedy that combines poppies with vinegar. Because of these medicinal uses, the poppy became associated with consoling the sick in the Victorian language of flowers.

PURPLE CLOVER

Trifolium pratense

Provident, prudent

• ◇ • ◇ • ◇ • ◇ •

Purple clover was one of many plants considered to have magical properties by early civilizations. Druids of the ancient Celtic cultures believed that a four-leaf clover was a talisman of good luck, helping a person to see evil spirits and ward them off. In medieval England, four-leaf clovers were emblems of the cross and thought to be good omens. In Irish folklore, clovers were said to be capable of rendering witches powerless and detecting fairies.

In Katharine Beals's 1917 *Flower Lore and Legend*, she relates another European fable that says whenever a fairy foot touched the ground, a four-leaved clover that was "possessed of magical power" would spring up. On the more romantic side of superstition, Beals shares an English song about two-leaf clovers:

> *A clover, a clover of two,*
> *Put in your right shoe,*
> *The first young man you meet,*
> *In field, street, or lane,*
> *You'll have him or one of his name.*

The purple clover, sometimes called red clover, is a member of the Fabaceae family, to which legumes, peas, and beans belong. It is native to Europe, Asia, and Africa and has flowers that grow into a purple to reddish-pink color; they can also be white and sometimes yellow. Clover grows freely

in the wild and has often been cultivated as a nutritious feed for livestock. It is also a large source of nectar for honeybees. Additionally, it is one of the few plants that transforms itself at night, with the two side leaves folding down together and the top center leaf bending over them, as if in prayer.

Another species of clover that was popular in English gardens was *Trifolium incarnatum*, the crimson clover. This clover has dark-red coloring with a more elongated bloom. In Victorian gardening journals, clovers were often grouped in discussion with grasses or edible plants such as mustard and peas. Although there aren't any specific examples of clover in an arrangement, grasses were frequently employed as a base, decorative edge, or filler in ornamental displays.

In Kate Greenaway's *The Language of Flowers*, she lists white clover as a symbol for "think of me," but no explanation is given for this association. In Henry Phillips's *Floral Emblems*, he explains that a responsible farmer "lays up a good store of clover for the subsistence of his cattle during the winter months," which is why clover is a symbol of this virtue. No symbols are given for the yellow clover.

PIGS IN CLOVER

In 1889 the American inventor and toy maker Charles Martin Crandall whose factory was based in Waverly, New York, released Pigs in Clover, a handheld game in which the player must manipulate marbles through a set of concentric circles to collect them within a center holding pen. The idea was that the pigs (marbles) had escaped from home (center holding area) so that they could feast on clovers in the field (the outer rings) and the farmer (the player) must round them back up. The game was so popular that, according to an 1889 article published in *The Waverly Free Press*, the toy factory was "turning out eight thousand 'Pigs in Clover' a day and [was] twenty days behind in orders." More recently, the game saw a resurgence in popularity after an altered version of it had been featured as a plot device in the science fiction television show *Westworld* (2016), based on the 1973 film of the same name that had been written and directed by author Michael Crichton.

RANUNCULUS

Ranunculus asiaticus

anunculus is an ancient wild meadow flower that has been cultivated for many centuries. This species, *Ranunculus asiaticus*, is commonly known as the Persian buttercup and is noteworthy for the ability of some of its varieties, such as the Bloomingdale or Tecolote Giant, to grow a large double flower that resembles a peony. Because of its fuller appearance and larger variety of colors, this species is much more popular with florists than the standard buttercup.

The Latin root of *ranunculus* is *rana*, which means "frog." In Beals's *Flower Lore and Legend*, she writes that this name "was given in ancient times because it so often grew in places where frogs sing." Ranunculus is sometimes called bachelor's buttons because of the plant's round bulbous root, which, during medieval times, was thought to be an effective treatment against the plague. According to Roman philosopher Apuleius (c. AD 12–170), hanging the roots in a linen cloth around the neck was a "sure cure for lunacy."

A commonly shared origin story of the the flower is the tale of Ranunculus, a handsome young Libyan man noted for his melodious voice and fine clothing of green and yellow silks. One day while out walking through the woods, he was singing to the woodland nymphs when, according to Beals, "he became so entranced with his own music that he expired in ecstasy and Orpheus [the Greek hero and musician] transformed him into the brilliant little flower."

In *Rapin of Gardens* (1728), the English translation of French writer Rapin's poem "Hortorum libri quattuor" (1672), he also writes of the ranunculus as a sweet-voiced Libyan youth who is inexplicably turned into a flower:

> Ranunculus *who with melodious Strains,*
> *Once charm'd the ravish'd Nymphs on* Libyan *Plains,*
> *Now boasts through verdant Fields his rich Attire,*
> *Whose love-sick Look betrays a secret Fire;*
> *Himself his Song beguil'd, and feiz'd his Mind*
> *With pleasing Flames for other Hearts design'd.*

In Henry Phillips's *Flora Historica*, he writes that the Persian buttercup, known at the time as *Tarobolos catamarlale*, had been cultivated in Constantinople by the Turks for several centuries before reaching Europe. The Turks' first encounter with this flower was through Cara Mustapha, a vizier (a high-ranking advisor during Ottoman rule) who noticed a neglected flower in the garden of the seraglio, the living quarters of the sultan's wives. Because Cara Mustapha hoped to "inspire the reigning sultan with a taste for plants similar to his own, he decorated the gardens of the Seraglio with this new flower." The flower attracted the sultan's attention; he soon ordered that all known ranunculus varieties to be found in the east be brought to him. He carefully preserved these ranunculi in the garden at the seraglio, where they remained unseen and inaccessible to the rest of the world. One day, the flowers were taken by an unknown thief and spread throughout the courts of Europe.

In Phillips's *Floral Emblems*, he refers to Persian buttercup as a common garden ranunculus and says that "ranunculus excel all flowers in the richness of their colours," which is why he assigned it the meaning "you are rich in attractions." This also explains why Elizabeth Washington Wirt chose to assign ranunculus the meaning of being dazzled by another's charms. The ranunculus was a highly popular flower to cultivate during the Victorian era. An article from *The Gardener's Chronicle* of 1847 describes a successfully grown plant as follows: "like the sun emerging from the east in a spring morning, the full orbed Ranunculus bursts upon the view."

• ◇ • ◇ • ◇ • ◇ •

Bright as the sun, her eyes the gazers strike,

And, like the sun, they shine on all alike.

—ALEXANDER POPE
The Rape of the Lock, canto 2, 1712

A Symbol of Resurrection

The Persian buttercup is a drought-tolerant wildflower that is often found growing naturally throughout Israel. Because of its ability to survive in the harsh, dry conditions, many people in Israel refer to it as the resurrection plant. To uncover what makes this flower so heat- and drought-resistant, Rina Kamenetsky, a researcher at Israel's Volcani Institute, discovered that, when the cells of the storage roots were viewed under a microscope, they very closely resemble the six-pointed star known as the Seal of Solomon among Muslims, or the Star of David in Judaism. This structure prevents the roots from being flooded with water in the winter but simultaneously allows it to store enough water to sustain itself for prolonged periods. In Hebrew, the Star of David is also known as the Shield of David, which Kemenetsky says is a "good description of how this plant's root-cell structure works" because it's capable of shielding itself from harm.

RHODODENDRON

Rhododendron

I shall never look upon your like again

• ◊ • ◊ • ◊ • ◊ •

Rhododendrons grow in many colors, but the most popular in Victorian-era gardening was the purple *Rhododendron maximum*, which *Flora's Dictionary* refers to as "the most distinguished variety." Rhododendrons are also toxic. It's because of this that Henry Phillips chose to assign "danger" to the rhododendron in his book *Floral Emblems*.

Rhododendrons are an ancient species of woody, flowering, evergreen plant of the Ericaceae family. They are primarily found growing in Asia and are a part of the *Rhododendron* genus, which also contains azaleas. The word *rhododendron* comes from the ancient Greek words *rhódon*, meaning "rose," and *déndron*, meaning "tree." Rhododendrons and azaleas should not be planted near walnut, pecan, or hickory trees. These trees produce compounds that are toxic to the roots of both plants.

Although rhododendrons are cultivated throughout the United States, they do not naturally occur in the Great Plains, Interior Plains, or Mexico. They primarily grow in Virginia and North Carolina and are widespread throughout the Appalachian Mountains, as well as the Pacific Northwest between the Cascade Mountains and the Pacific Ocean.

According to *The Gardener's Chronicle* of 1841, not only was the rhododendron extremely easy to grow, even seeding itself when planted in the woods, it also made excellent shelter for small game, which could be useful if one were looking to attract such animals. Additionally, the magazine notes that, as an evergreen, the rhododendron was appreciated for its year-round "delightful appearances in dreary weather," and that "when in bloom, nothing can surpass the beauty of rhododendrons in woods." In *Flora's Dictionary*, Elizabeth Washington Wirt exclaims that "with the exception of the Magnolia, [rhododendrons] are decidedly the most magnificent flowering trees, that any country can boast." She elaborates on its symbolism by adding, "our lofty mountains, deep ravines, and rocky precipices, present to the eye of the traveller, an assemblage of beauty, truly astonishing—but this, pre-eminent above the rest, arrests his progress—he pauses in mute wonderment—and, in the lingering look of admiration, as he proceeds, he feels that he *ne'er shall look upon its like again.*"

There is not much in the way of lore or superstition surrounding the rhododendron; however, like Wirt, garden journalists were inspired by its beauty. The 1889 issue of *The Gardeners' Chronicle* describes its charm and constant variability: "resulting in that endless variety, that marvellous complexity, and that exquisite colouring which excite our admiration in the realm of flowers and constitute them the perennial charm and crowning glory of Nature."

Transcendentalist Ralph Waldo Emerson's poem "The Rhodora" (1834) celebrates the plant as well as it demonstrates his belief that nature exists to satisfy the soul without rhyme or reason. He writes:

> *Rhodora! if the sages ask thee why*
> *This charm is wasted on the earth and sky,*
> *Tell them, dear, that, if eyes were made for seeing,*
> *Then beauty is its own excuse for Being;*
> *Why thou wert there, O rival of the rose!*
> *I never thought to ask; I never knew;*
> *But in my simple ignorance suppose*
> *The self-same power that brought me there, brought you.*

Rhododendrons were primarily admired for their outdoor ornamental charm, while the azalea, because of its variety of color, was used more often for indoor arrangements. In Annie Hassard's *Floral Decorations for the Dwelling House*, she includes rhododendron in the seasonal blooming flowers of May, June, July, and August, with the note at the end of the list that these are intended as a rough guide for arrangements.

• ◇ • ◇ • ◇ • ◇ •

The blaze of Rhod. flowers and various colored jungle proclaims a differently constituted region in a naturalist's eye & twenty species here, to one there, always are asking me the vexed question, where do we come from?

—JOSEPH DALTON HOOKER
Letter to Charles Darwin, June 24, 1849

Azaleas versus Rhododendrons

It's easy to confuse azaleas and rhododendrons. They have a very similar appearance and their names are often used interchangeably in gardening stores. Below are a few characteristics that can help you tell them apart more easily.

AZALEAS	RHODODENDRONS
Five stamens	Ten stamens
Funnel-shaped flowers	Bell-shaped flowers
Small, sometimes hairy leaves	Large, fleshy leaves
Will only have clusters of one to three flowers on the end of a stem	Will have large, crowded clusters on the edge of a stem
All azaleas are rhododendrons	Not all rhododendrons are azaleas
Many azaleas are deciduous, and shed their leaves each fall, with two species as the exceptions: *R. mucronulatum* and *R. dauricum*.	Most rhododendrons are evergreen and do not shed their leaves.

ROSE

Rosa

FULL-BLOWN PINK ROSE: Engagement
HALF-BLOWN PINK ROSE: Love
JAPANESE ROSE: Grace
PINK ROSEBUD: Admiration
MOSS ROSE: Superior merit
MOSS ROSEBUD: Confession
MUSK ROSE: Charm
RED ROSE: Deep modesty
WHITE ROSE: I am worthy of you
WHITE ROSEBUD: A heart that is ignorant of love
YELLOW ROSE: The decrease of love on better acquaintance
YORK AND LANCASTER ROSE: War

• ◇ • ◇ •◇ • ◇ •

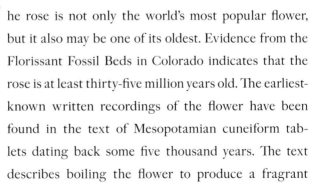

The rose is not only the world's most popular flower, but it also may be one of its oldest. Evidence from the Florissant Fossil Beds in Colorado indicates that the rose is at least thirty-five million years old. The earliest-known written recordings of the flower have been found in the text of Mesopotamian cuneiform tablets dating back some five thousand years. The text describes boiling the flower to produce a fragrant water for some unknown purpose, yet it stresses using only very small quantities due to its preciousness.

In his ancient herbal book *De Materia Medica*, Greek physician Pedanius Dioscorides wrote that roses possessed astringent qualities that made them useful for cleaning and healing wounds. He also gave instructions on how to prepare rose oil to help with skin disorders. He wrote that roses, if boiled in water then ingested, could help with headaches, earaches, problems with the eyes, gums, ulcers, and maternal pains. Today, the rose is still cultivated for its curative and beautifying properties: rose oil is a highly sought-after ingredient for perfume and cosmetics—and it's expensive to produce. It can take up to sixty thousand roses to produce just one ounce.

Over the ages, there have been countless superstitions and folk stories, mostly from ancient Greek and Roman mythology, about the rose and its magical or medicinal properties. In both cultures, there is a strong relationship between the rose and Aphrodite (Venus), the goddess of love. Some versions of the Greek myth of her birth say that when Aphrodite was born, the foam that dripped from her body as she ascended from the sea turned into white roses. This is depicted in Sandro Botticelli's painting *The Birth of Venus*, where roses can be seen swirling around Venus and descending from her floating scallop shell as she approaches land.

In the Greek story of Aphrodite and Adonis, both Aphrodite, goddess of love, and Persephone, goddess of the underworld, are in love with the beautiful young human, Adonis. One day Adonis goes on a hunt and is gored by a wild boar sent by one of the many jealous or angry gods that have an agenda against Aphrodite. Hearing the news, Aphrodite rushes to Adonis. As he bleeds to death in her arms, she cries, her tears falling onto a wild white rose growing nearby and staining it red. This is the story of how we came to have red roses. In another version shared by Elizabeth Washington Wirt, Aphrodite was pricked by the thorn of a white rose bush while rushing to her dying Adonis. Her blood fell onto one of the roses and turned them red. In the story of Aphrodite and Adonis in Book X of Ovid's *Metamorphoses*, the flower created was said to be an anemone, a type of ranunculus, but over the years, through poetry and retellings, various storytellers have replaced it with the rose.

In both Greek and Roman mythology, the rose has been associated with Aphrodite and her son Eros, the god of love and attraction. In one unnamed

CLEOPATRA'S CARPET

While trying to impress her lover, Marc Antony, Cleopatra held extravagant festivals for several days when she went to visit him in the ancient Mediterranean city of Cilicia. According to American landscape architect Samuel B. Parsons's 1908 *Parsons on the Rose*, on the fourth day of her visit she purchased a "talent worth" of roses, an amount that would roughly equal $1.25 million in modern estimates. She used them to carpet the floor of one of the halls at a depth of eighteen inches. Later in their relationship, when Marc Antony received the false news that Cleopatra had killed herself, he chose to do the same and impaled himself on his sword. As he was dying, he was taken to her and asked her to cover his tomb in roses.

story, Eros gave a rose to Harpocrates, the god of silence, to ensure all indiscretions of Aphrodite and the other gods would remain secret. For this reason, up through the Middle Ages, the rose was considered a symbol of secrecy. Roses were often either suspended from the ceiling or carved into ceilings above tables to remind everyone present that what was said at the table should be kept confidential. The Latin term *sub rosa*, meaning "under the rose," is an old phrase meaning "secrecy;" it was first recorded in Edmund Gayton's *Pleasant Notes upon Don Quixot* (1654).

In the sixteenth century, a red rose was chosen as a central plot device in what is now a classic love story: Gabrielle-Suzanne Barbot de Villeneuve's *Beauty and the Beast* (1704). When Belle's father sets off on a trip, she asks him to bring her a rose as a gift in lieu of expensive dresses or jewels. It is his procurement of the flower that sets off a chain of events that result in her falling in love with the Beast.

Beloved for centuries, the rose became a prominent bloom in the Victorian flower lexicon because of its beauty, fragrance, ease of cultivation, range of colors, and romantic allusions. Flowers that came in pink or white varieties were particularly popular for their suggestions of sweetness, femininity, and purity, which only added to the appeal of the many varieties of rose. Additionally, any rose that had a strong scent or a large bloom was highly admired.

In Victorian England, the moss rose was an extremely popular variety in the garden because it grows in a wide array of colors and is relatively easy to cultivate. In fact, some gardening manuals suggest that there are very few ways to kill a moss rose. Introduced to England from the Netherlands during the sixteenth century, the flower's moss-covered stem intrigued and enchanted gardeners, who were drawn to—and highly valued—its beauty and fragrance. In Henry Phillips's *Floral Emblems*, he describes the moss rose as the rose "on which Flora has bestowed so many of her choicest gifts." Considered at the time to be one of the best examples of what a rose should be, it's not surprising that the moss rose came to signify "superior merit." In other words, as a feature in a bouquet, the moss rose might suggest that the admirer considers the recipient to be superior above all others.

In addition to their species and color, roses were thought to have significance based on their stages of bloom. Cited as a resource for helping to craft the rose list in *Flora's Dictionary, The Memoirs of Signor Gaudentio di Lucca* was an anonymously published work of fiction often attributed to Bishop George Berkeley, an Irish philosopher during the Age of Reason (1685–1815).

Whom Will I Marry?

According to *Popular Romances of the West of England* (1881), a medieval English superstition from Cornwall suggested that a rose could be used to learn the identity of a young woman's future husband. On a midsummer evening, the woman needed to walk backward into her garden and pick a rose, then carefully sew it up inside a paper bag and leave it in a drawer untouched until Christmas morning, when she was to open the bag in complete silence, pin the rose to her chest, and wear it to church. It was thought that a young man would come and ask for the rose or possibly take it from her without asking. Whoever took the rose was thought to be her future husband.

This was an important time in the development of European intellectualism and philosophy that overlapped the onset of the Victorian era and later influenced many Victorian attitudes. In this story, Mezzorama exists as a place described as a utopia. Here, the rose has symbolism depending on the state of its bloom. The rise and progress of love between a lover and his mistress is expressed by a rosebud as it goes from a closed to a fully opened state. First, admiration is expressed with a mostly closed rosebud. After making a closer acquaintance, the half-blown rose is presented. Finally, the full acceptance of love is represented by a full-blown rose, which is considered an engagement for life. In *Floral Emblems*, Phillips refers to full-blown roses as the "queen" or "pride of Flora."

Regarding Victorian bouquets, wearing floral crowns was considered an out-of-date pagan practice and thus frowned upon. A flower as a small decoration on the hair or dress however, was common. Roses were a favored decoration for brides and bridal parties, with the bride sometimes receiving a bouquet consisting only of white roses and camellias.

Today, there are hundreds of species of roses, with thousands of hybrids being developed each year. They continue to be extremely popular gardening plants and are not only frequently included in weddings year-round, but in bouquets for all occasions, whether somber or celebratory. About half of today's species originate from Asia, with the remaining half divided equally from North America and Europe, although extensive hybridization and cross-breeding makes it nearly impossible to identify their origins in most cases.

• ◇ • ◇ • ◇ • ◇ •

On their best side let's see things:
You complain of seeing thorny roses;
I rejoice and give thanks to the gods
The thorns have roses.

—ALPHONSE KARR
Lettres écrites de mon jardin (Letters written from my garden), 1853

THE TUDOR ROSE

The red rose was the emblem for the English royal House of Lancaster, and the white, the emblem of Lancaster's rival, the House of York. The War of the Roses (1455–1487) was a civil battle between the two Houses in which Henry VII (of the House of Tudor but fighting for the House of Lancaster), defeated Richard III of the House of York. Later, Henry VII married Elizabeth of York. To symbolize the unification of the houses, Henry created a hybrid from the red and white roses, what we know today as the Tudor rose, an emblem that applies to heraldic use only. In the Victorian language of flowers, the Tudor rose is represented by the red-and-white variegated York and Lancaster rose. Although the Tudor rose was created as a symbol of unity and Wirt believed that its beauty "prettily typified" this peace, she felt that the red-and-white variegated rose brought to mind thoughts of war nonetheless. The Tudor rose is still used in English heraldry to this day, representing England in a more general sense.

With King Henry VIII ascending to the throne upon his father's death, the Tudor period was well under way. Henry, infamous for the dissolution of six marriages, was a man of great appetites. He liked receiving gifts depicting or relating to roses, especially those made of gold. During the exchange of gifts at the New Year in January 1532, he received from the Earl of Shrewsbury a nine-ounce gold flagon for rosewater and, from Goron Bartinis, a member of the court, a golden ring fashioned like a rose.

It has also been customary for Catholic popes to gift distinguished organizations, people, or members of royal families with golden roses. This is done as a simultaneous token of respect and a symbol of spiritual substance. In 1524, Henry received from a group of ambassadors to Pope Clement VII "a tree forged of fine gold, & wrought with branches, leaus, and floures resembling roses. This tree was set in a pot of gold which had three feet of antique fashion. The pot was of measure halfe a pint, in the uppermost rose was a faire saphire loupe persed, the bignesse of an acorne, the tree was of height halfe an English yard, and a foot in bredth." A few of these golden roses given by popes still exist today, but what became of Henry's magnificent tree is unknown.

Snapdragon

Antirrhinum

Presumption

. ◊ . ◊ . ◊ . ◊ .

ccording to Irish gardener and journalist William Robinson, snapdragons were not only easy to cultivate, but also quite hardy and popular in the English Victorian garden. The most favored varieties were those with solid-colored flowers that looked striking from any distance.

The snapdragon gets its name from the fact that, when the sides of the flower are squeezed, they resemble a dragon opening and closing its mouth, with the stamen resembling a tongue. After the flowers have bloomed and fallen off, the seed pods that are left behind resemble skulls. The flower's genus name, *Antirrhinum*, is taken from the Greek word *antirrhinon*, which roughly translates as "cow's snout." In Victorian flower books, comparisons are made to both dragon and calf snouts, and Henry Phillips's *Floral Emblems* refers to the countenance as a "mask," making it an appropriate symbol for presumption. The snapdragon is a plant of the Plantaginaceae, or plantain, family and native to North America, Europe, and Africa. It is within the order Lamiales, making it a relative to herbs and plants such as lavender, jasmine, olive, sesame, and basil, among many others.

In T. F. Dyer's *The Folklore of Plants*, he recounts an English superstition of wearing snapdragon with dill and flax as a talisman to protect against sorcery and witchcraft. He writes that it had been believed that snapdragon had the ability to break or destroy charms, along with other unspecified magical abilities. In a related north German superstition, it was believed that a bouquet containing snapdragon, blue marjoram, black cumin, a right shirt sleeve, and a left stocking could be placed in a baby's crib to protect the child from the Nickert, a small gray person who lived in water and had a strong desire to steal unbaptized human babies and replace them with his own large-headed children.

In the ancient herbal book *De Materia Medica*, Dioscordes wrote that, when worn as an ornament, snapdragon could prevent injury from poison and when rubbed into the skin with lily oil or cyprine, it would make one beautiful. Henry Lyte's *A niewe Herball*, which lists the snapdragon, compares the appearance of the flower to a frog's mouth and explains a superstition that says carrying snapdragon will protect the bearer from harm, injury, venom, or poison. Another medicinal use he suggests is to add any "decoction" of snapdragons to bathwater to remove any yellowness from one's body after having jaundice.

Snapdragons were valuable in the Victorian garden as tall ornamental flowers that added a pop of color, particularly when planted behind smaller flowers. They were often shown in exhibitions and would even occasionally appear in a winter garden if the weather remained mild enough. They were not common in daily bouquets or arrangements. Because of their long stalks, they're better suited to taller indoor arrangements.

• ◇ • ◇ • ◇ • ◇ •

Presumption should never make us neglect that which appears easy to us, nor despair make us lose courage at the sight of difficulties.

—STANISŁAW LESZCZYŃSKI
"Reflections on Different Subjects of Morality," *The Universal Magazine*, 1765

Posies, Tussie-Mussies, and Nosegays

In the late Victorian era, sweetly scented flowers were used extensively in perfumes in addition to bouquets, or "posies," small bunches of flowers arranged based on color and layered according to size and texture. In addition to being held in the hand, they were used as decoration for hats, dresses, and jackets. Posies were sometimes referred to as "tussie-mussies," which would usually contain herbs, or nosegays, which were small bunches of sweet- or happy-smelling flowers.

A popular Victorian accessory, the posy holder was a small and often intricately decorated handheld funnel-shaped container with an attached pin that could secure a few flowers at a time. A long chain with a ring on the end allowed the carrier to attach the posy to her hand so that it could swing freely while she danced. Some designs included a loop on the end of the holder so that a ribbon could be tied through it instead. In G. Bernard Hughes's 1952 book *More About Collecting Antiques*, he notes that sweet-smelling flower bouquets had been used for centuries as a portable way to shield one's nose from unpleasant fragrances while out and about. The fine gloves and dresses worn by women in the 1700s necessitated the invention of a bouquet holder, which they called *porte-fleur* (flower holder, in French). Although Hughes writes that the *porte-fleur* was introduced to England by the German Hanoverian Court, one of the earliest-known designs was a tube of slender gold made by the London jeweler H. Pugh, at Raquette Court, Fleet Street, in the late 1730s. Sometimes these holders were made into brooches that could be worn more easily on the lapel of a jacket. A later update to the posy holder design known as a *bouquetier* incorporated jewels around the top of the flute and sometimes included a tiny mirror that was applied to the surface so that a woman may discreetly examine her surroundings at a party.

SNOWDROP

Galanthus nivalis

Hope or consolation

he snowdrop, with its pendulum-like white flower, is one of the first to bloom at the end of winter, making it a harbinger of spring. Native to Europe and the Middle East, it has been known to grow in large numbers in the woods. Its name, *Galanthus nivalis*, comes from *galanthus*, the Greek word for milk, and *ánthos*, the Greek word for flower. The plant was named by botanist Carl Linnaeus in *Species Plantarum* as an allusion to the flower's milky-white coloring. The word *nivalis* is rooted in the Latin, meaning "snowy" or "of snow." The snowdrop is an ancient member of the Amaryllidaceae family, making it a direct relative of the daffodil.

Victorians assigned the snowdrop the emblem of consolation because it's "the first flower that awakes from the repose of winter and cheers us with the assurance of the reanimation of nature," according to *Floral Emblems*. Other Victorian books and magazines referred to the flower as refined and old-fashioned but also beautiful, chaste, and sentimental.

According to Henry Lyte's *A niewe Herball*, the snowdrop was originally described by the Greek philosopher Theophrastus (371–287 BC) in *Enquiry into Plants* as a white, bulbous violet, which he called *Leucoion* or *Viola alba*. Lyte himself also referred to it as the white, bulbus violet or the narcissus violet, but was unfamiliar with any medicinal qualities it might possess. In the

1633 revised edition of the botanist John Gerarde's *The herball, or, Generall historie of plantes*, editor Thomas Johnson describes Theophrastus's white violet and says that it grows abundantly in the woods of Italy and that some call it "snow drops." This seems to be the first recorded use of the name snowdrop. At this time Johnson was also unfamiliar with any useful applications for this flower other than being "maintained and cherished in gardens for the beautie and rarenesse of the floures, and sweetnesse of their smell."

In Homer's *Odyssey*, the god Hermes gives Odysseus an antidote to the goddess Circe's poisons, which he calls "moly." According to the medical paper "Homer's Moly Identified as *Galanthus Nivalis L.*: Physiologic Antidote to Stramonium Poisoning," written for the March 1983 issue of *The Clinical Neuropharmacology*, it's believed that this mention of moly may have been a reference to the snowdrop. This hypothesis is further substantiated by a separate identical description of "moly" and its uses in Pedanius Dioscorides's *De Materia Medica*. In addition to this being the earliest-known recording of the snowdrop for the treatment of neurological conditions, it has since been discovered that this flower, along with a few other members of the Amaryllidaceae family, contain an alkaloid called galantamine. In modern medicine, galantamine has shown to be effective in treating muscular and neurological effects of polio and Alzheimer's disease.

In Romania, the ancient festival Mărțișor celebrates the start of spring on March 1. On that day, it is customary for a man to give a small bunch of snowdrops as a gift to a woman. There are also a number of legends associated with this holiday. In one, the sun takes the form of a beautiful youth so that it can come down to the village and dance with the people. A monster kidnaps it, locking it in a cold, dark dungeon, where its warmth and light cannot escape. The world became very sad at this loss. Then, one day, a strong young man decides he will free the sun. He sets out on a journey that lasts the length of summer, fall, and winter. He arrives at the dungeon and, with the ground covered in snow, he fights the monster and frees the sun. During the battle, wherever his blood drips, the snow melts and a snowdrop grows and blooms in its place immediately, signaling the arrival of spring. As the man dies, he is happy to see the sun ascending back toward the sky.

According to Thomas Miller's 1860 *Common Wayside Flowers*, there is an old-world English tale about the origin of snowdrops and how they became the emblem for hope. In it, a personification of hope, with spring standing beside her, looks down at earth, watching a winter snowfall. Hope then tells spring that the earth would be so much more cheerful if the snowflakes were turned into white flowers. With a smile, spring blows a warm breath onto the falling snow and turns the flakes into blooms. Hope catches the first flower as it falls, saying that "it should be her emblem throughout all time."

She then says:

Oftimes, when thou art gone,
I'm left alone, without a thing
That I can fix my heart upon,
For Winter's lonely without Spring.
'Twill cheer me now for many an hour,
And in the future I shall see
Those who would sink raised by this flower—
'Twill make them think of thee and me;
And many a sadful heart will sing,
The snowdrop bringeth Hope and Spring.

So if you're ever feeling a bit down from the winter weather blues, just keep an eye out for snowdrops and know that spring will be here soon. It's certainly more predictable than the appearance of a groundhog's shadow! Clearly, the snowdrop has a special place on the list of life's simple pleasures.

SNOWDROP AS MUSE

Many poets were inspired by the appearance of this delicate harbinger of spring. Lord Alfred Tennyson's poem "The Snowdrop" cheerfully describes the appearance of the "fair-maid":

Many, many welcomes,
February fair-maid,
Ever as of old time,
Solitary firstling,
Coming in the cold time,
Prophet of the gay time,
Prophet of the May time,
Prophet of the roses,
Many, many welcomes,
February fair-maid!

In Lewis Morris's poem "The Epic of Hades" (1885), a snowdrop symbolizes hope for the narrator, who has just escaped Hades and arrived in a barren field back on Earth:

And as I went
Across the lightening fields, upon a bank
I saw a single Snowdrop glance, and bring
Promise of spring.

Finally, in Robert Williams Buchanan's poem "Poet Andrew" (1866), the appearance of a snowdrop is described as a thing of awesome beauty:

Could you understand
One who was wild as if he found a mine
Of golden guineas, when he noticed first
The soft green streaks in a snowdrop's inner leaves?

SUNFLOWER

Helianthus annuus

Haughtiness

• ◇ • ◇ • ◇ • ◇ •

unflowers are native to North and South America and were commonly grown by Native Americans as a food crop and may have been domesticated as a food source earlier than corn—even as early as 1000 BC. One of the oldest flower fossil records was found in Río Pichileufú, Argentina; it was a 47.5-million-year-old sunflower species that is now extinct.

The leaves, petals, and seeds of the sunflower are edible, and the seeds were often eaten by the Native Americans as a snack, ground into flour for baking, and pressed for oil. The oil was used for food as well as to moisturize the hair and skin. They would also dry out the stalks and use them as a building material, although the exact applications are unspecified. During the Spanish colonization of the Americas, the sunflower was discovered and brought back to Spain in 1510. Unaware of its culinary uses at this time, the Spanish thought of it as an exotic ornamental plant and it gained popularity throughout Europe on that basis.

The sunflower's Latin name, *Helianthus*, is from the Greek word *hēlios* (sun) and *anthos* (flower) and was given for the flower's tilting movement toward the sun. It's been said that the affection the sunflower has for the sun contributed to the symbolism associated with it, because its adoration of the sun could be interpreted as that of a "fawning courtier," according to T. F. Dyer.

In John Gerarde's *The herball, or, Generall historie of plantes*, he refers to the sunflower as "Indian Sun," "Floure of the Sun," "Marigold of Peru," "Flos Solis Maior" (Latin for "large sunflower"), and finally "Sun-Floure." He explains that it was given this name for its tendency to turn toward the sun, but notes that he was never able to observe this behavior himself and thinks the flower was so named because it "resembles the radiant beams of the Sunne." He describes the sunflowers from his own garden growing to a height of fourteen feet tall with flowers spanning sixteen inches and having the overall smell of turpentine.

Gerarde also points out that the ancient writers hadn't recorded any medicinal uses for the plant but that he had found through personal trial and error "that the buds before they be floured boiled and eaten with butter, vinegar, and pepper, after the manner of Artichokes, are exceeding pleasant meat, surpassing the Artichoke far in procuring bodily lust." Additionally, he had tried eating the buds, with the tops of the stalks attached, broiled on a griddle and dressed with oil, vinegar, and pepper and found it to have a similar taste. For the Jerusalem artichoke, he describes a similar preparation, only with the addition of ginger, and another where they can be added to pie with bone marrow, dates, ginger, and raisins.

Later, around 1860, Russia began cultivating large crops of sunflowers for their seed oil because it was one of the few sources of fat that the Russian Orthodox Church permitted its congregation to eat during Lent. After this time, publications began to write about sunflowers being gardened for their seeds as well as their decorative qualities. The 1891 edition of *The Gardeners' Chronicle* mentions this, citing in particular the Chiswick House Gardens of London, created and designed by Richard Boyle and landscape architect William Kent in the 1720s. Chiswick is where architecture and gardens inspired by ancient Rome gave birth to the English Landscape Movement during the nineteenth century. This, according to the Chiswick Gardens Trust, was one of the greatest influences on European art, architecture, and gardening, including the gardens at Blenheim Palace in Oxfordshire and Central Park in New York City.

In modern medicine, sunflower seed oil has been discovered to be high in vitamin E and oleic acid and proven to have a positive impact in helping reduce cholesterol, inflammation from arthritis, and constipation, and as a topical aid for healing wounds.

Like the chrysanthemum and dahlia, the sunflower is a member of the very old and large Asteraceae family. In *Flora's Dictionary*, Elizabeth Washington Wirt mentions two types of commonly cultivated sunflowers, *Helianthus indicus*, a smaller "Dwarf" variety, and *Helianthus annuus*, the larger variety. She describes the smaller sunflower as symbolic of adoration and the larger sunflower as haughtiness, but she gives no explanation as to why. She does offer the detail of how ancient Peruvians used the sunflower in ceremonies to worship their sun god. The virgin officiators would wear crowns made of solid-gold sunflowers while carrying bunches of fresh sunflowers held to their breasts.

In Ovid's *Metamorphoses*, he tells the story of how the water nymph Clytie was transformed into a sunflower by the sun god, Helios. Clytie had been in love with Helios but he abandoned her for her sister, Leucothoe. In her anger, Clytie tells their father of the affair and he, in turn, has Leucothoe put to death. Because Clytie's actions resulted in the death of his lover, Helios no longer wants anything to do with her. Clytie is distraught and she mourns the loss of Helios's affections by stripping herself naked and sitting on a rock for nine days, doing nothing but staring at the sun. Without food or water, she wastes away, becoming a pale flower that clings to the earth, only moving her face slightly whenever the sun passes by in the sky. Ovid's story was originally told with Clytie transforming into a *Heliotropium*, but by the seventeenth century, the story was often told such that she transformed into a sunflower due to its heliotropism (behavior of following the sun) and its resemblance to the sun itself.

THE JUDGMENT OF FLOWERS

One of the more celebrated flower books produced during the Victorian era, *Les Fleurs Animées* (The Flowers Personified) by French caricaturist Jean-Jacques Grandville (1803–1847), was first published posthumously in 1847. The book is remarkable: it opens with a gorgeous page that spells out the book title on a stalk from which hang single delicately colored blossoms, each in the shape of a letter. The book is filled with personified flowers dressed in clever costumes composed of their natural blossoms. Today a copy in very good condition can sell for thousands of dollars.

The book's short stories offer a satirical examination of personality types and the social mores of the day. In the first story, "The Flower Fairy," a procession of all the flower species arrives at a fairy's palace to ask permission to assume human form. They are tired of their flower life and wish to "judge for ourselves whether that which they say above, of our character, is agreeable to truth" so that the flowers may experience the virtues so often bestowed upon them in art and poetry. The flowers argue that these works would not exist if it weren't for them and wish to see if the language representing them in the human world is truly their own. The short stories that follow the fairy's grant of this wish relate each flower's adventures as a means of social observation and commentary.

In the story of the sunflower, "The Last Cacique," set in the mid-1700s in Mexico City, we are introduced to Tumilco who is a cacique, a leader of one of the many indigenous tribes in Mexico. The Inquisition, a part of the Catholic Church, despises the caciques for their "heretical" worshipping of the sun. In

an effort to appease the Inquisition, the governor of Mexico City plans to publicly burn a cacique at the stake and captures Tumilco. Minutes before he is to be burned at the stake, Tumilco's life is spared in exchange for his agreement to a public baptism and conversion to Christianity. With the new Christian name of Esteban, Tumilco is no longer a happily wandering indigenous hunter but a permanent Christian citizen of Mexico City.

One day after he has fallen very ill, he asks a neighbor to send a physician but is instead sent a priest. Although the priest tries to get Esteban to think of God as he lays in bed dying, he insists that his name is Tumilco and that he has only ever worshipped the sun. As Tumilco watches the sun set through his window he exclaims, "There is my god, and the god of my fathers. Sun! Receive thy child to thy bosom!" Then he dies, and the neighbor who sent the priest eulogizes Tumilco: "Sooner might you prevent the sunflower from following the sun in his course, than one of these heretics from returning to the worship of their luminary. This is what we gained by not burning him." The narrator concludes that Tumilco was merely the incarnation of the sunflower; "in worshipping the sun, he did but obey the laws of his being."

Forcing the indigenous people of Mexico to observe Catholicism was ultimately counterintuitive and against their nature. Similarly, forcing a sunflower to stop looking at the sun would be an effort made in vain. Over the years, many poems have portrayed the sunflower as being proud or haughty, but its inherent nature is simply to observe and appreciate its natural surroundings and to stay true to itself.

Sweet Pea

Lathyrus odoratus

Delicate pleasure

• ◊ • ◊ • ◊ • ◊ •

The sweet pea is a flowering climbing plant of the Fabaceae family, to which beans, peas, and legumes belong. The plant has a fresh, cheerful fragrance but is toxic and should never be consumed. The sweet pea is native to Sicily and Sardinia. Sicilian monk and botanist Father Francesco Cupani wrote one of the earliest descriptions of the plant in *Syllabus plantarum Siciliae Nuper detectarum* (1695), which appears to be a log of recently discovered plant specimens on the island. He was so enthusiastic about the purple flower that he began to distribute its seeds among fellow botanists and, in 1699, sent some to the horticulturist Robert Uvedale in Enfield, England. This marked the arrival of the first sweet peas in the country.

A second type of rose-colored sweet pea is mentioned in Carl Linneaus's *Species Plantarum.* Native to Ceylon, India, this variety, sometimes referred to as the "painted lady," was sometimes thought by early botanists to be the true original specimen of sweet pea. There is little evidence to support that it was known before the Sicilian sweet pea from which the Victorian hybrids originated.

The earliest-known natural colors of the sweet pea were white, purple, red, and red with white, although only the purple and red varieties were identified definitively as being from Italy and India, respectively. As of 1793,

through the careful selection and breeding of these colors, new sweet pea varieties became available in yellows, blues, and a dark purplish black.

The Victorians adored sweet peas. In 1870, while employed as the head gardener for William Sankey at Sandywell in Gloucester, England, Scottish botanist Henry Eckford began trying to improve upon the sweet pea by crossing and intercrossing all known varieties. In 1882, at The Trial of Sweet Peas at Chiswick, Eckford was given his first award by the Floral Committee for his new sweet pea cultivar, the bronze prince. Unfortunately, reliable reproduction of this cultivar proved difficult and it completely disappeared shortly after its creation.

But all was not for naught. According to noted horticulturist Richard Dean in his 1900 book, *The Sweet Pea Bicentenary Celebration*, Eckford's work with sweet peas sparked a seemingly insatiable public appetite for new varieties each year. By 1898 at least twenty-two new varieties had been created. Eckford managed to improve not only upon the size and height of the plants, but also upon the variety of color. New colors ranged from white to "exquisite shades of cream and buff, to pale yellow," from "softest pinks up to rich rose" and a "dazzling scarlet," to "tones of lavender, dark blues, and even a variety of claret-purple sweet pea called 'Black Knight.'" Ultimately, Eckford's work led to most modern sweet pea varieties we know today and, even at the time of Dean's book, had earned him the unofficial nickname, The Sweet Pea King.

Well before Eckford's successes and the Victorian interest in the sweet pea intensified, Henry Phillips had already made it the emblem for "delicate pleasure" in *Floral Emblems* due to the "charms this flower displays in both fragrance and colour." In a modern bouquet, sweet peas can offer a romantic, delicate, and fun flourish because of their sweet fragrance, range of colors, and the ruffled butterfly-like appearance of the blossoms. They are often used in wedding bouquets and continue to be a popular garden ornamental.

THE SWEET PEA EXHIBITION

The Bicentenery Sweet Pea Exhibition was held on July 20 and 21, 1900, at the Crystal Palace in London, with the dual purpose of celebrating the sweet pea's introduction to England and creating a scheme for classifying the flowers at future shows. As a result, the National Sweet Pea Society was formed and has continued to hold annual sweet pea events in England to this day.

The categories at the Bicentenery included dinner-table decoration, baskets, wreaths, plain posies, really any creative way that an exhibitor might come up with that could show off the beauty of the sweet pea. There were three divisions involved for judging: Division I was for professional gardeners; Division II, for amateurs aided by one gardener; and Division III, for amateurs who cultivated their plants themselves. Each division also included "classes," or types of arrangements that were expected. Below is an example of a Division III call to entry and additional notes to keep in mind for all divisions.

DIVISION III.

Floral Decorations Of Sweet Peas—Open To All Class 30.

———

A table 12 feet by 6 feet, standing by itself, will be provided for each Exhibitor in this Class, the subjects which may be baskets, wreathes, posies, crosses, anchors, &c., to be arranged in any way the taste of the Exhibitor might suggest. Any appropriate light foliage may be employed, but the Sweet Pea blossoms only. Four Prizes—£5, £4, £3, £2.

——— ✳ ✳ ✳ ✳ ✳ ✳ ———

NOTE.—In all the forgoing Classes, except 11 and 12, each bunch must contain Twenty-five Sprays of one variety only. The term "bunch" is employed in its ordinary sense, and the stems need not necessarily be tied. Each bunch to be set up tastefully in a Vase. Grasses and Gypsophila may be employed as appropriate light foliage.

NOTE.—Suitable Vases will be provided by the Committee to secure uniformity as far as possible, but as the Committee will be put to considerable expense in providing them, the vases will be let out for use at a charge of One Penny each vase, on the Exhibitor undertaking to sign a contract to restore them, uninjured, to an appointed official at the close of the Exhibition.

Edinburgh Castle

THISTLE

Carduus

Intrusion

• ◇ • ◇ • ◇• ◇ •

The symbolism of the thistle was well established hundreds of years before the Victorian era. Popular Scottish legend has it that the country was under invasion by the Danes in the fifteenth century. At the time, it had been deemed unwarlike to attack an enemy at night, but one evening the Danes decided to ignore this edict and approached the Scottish forces under the cover of darkness and barefoot to muffle the sounds of their footsteps. Unfortunately for the Danes, the Scottish lands were covered in thistles, which caused the soldiers to cry out in surprise and pain, therefore alerting the sleeping Scottish forces to their approach. The thistle was immediately adopted as the national insignia, representing protection and bravery.

In 1470 King James III of Scotland ordered the thistle to be incorporated onto national coins. Later, the Order of the Thistle, an order of knighthood, was created. Its exact origins have been widely debated, with some sources believing it was created in 1540 by King James V of Scotland and others believing it was established in 1687 by King James II of England. Regardless, the order consisted of twelve knights all wearing badges depicting the thistle.

The thistle is a wild-growing, prickly, flowering herb that is native to Eurasia and Africa. Like the chrysanthemum, dahlia, and sunflower, it's also a member of the Asteraceae family. While the sunchoke (Jerusalem artichoke) is a type of sunflower, the commonly consumed globe artichoke is a type of thistle. Like sunflowers and artichokes, thistles are entirely edible, however, depending on the state of growth, they may not be very palatable. Younger thistles have more tender leaves and stalks, but the thorns cannot be removed from the buds until they're more mature.

There are a few different species of thistle with *Carduus*, *Cirsium*, and *Onopordum* most commonly considered to be true thistles. These are respectively known as the plumeless thistle, the Scotch (or common) thistle, and the cotton thistle; all three have a purple-colored flower. In Henry Lyte's *A niewe Herball*, he describes eleven kinds of thistle and five thistle-like plants associated with them. Of these, the "wilde thistel," which he says grows in all places of England in fields and meadows, seems closest to what we would know today as a common thistle. He describes boiling the root of the wild thistle in wine and drinking it as a remedy to cleanse the blood and urine and to "amendeth the stenche of the armepittes, and of all the rest of the body." Of the artichoke, he writes that, when eaten, it can be useful as both an aphrodisiac and fertility aid for both men and women.

The word *carduus* is from the Proto-Indo-European root *kars* meaning "to scratch, scrape, rub, card." In *Flora's Dictionary*, *carduus* is thought to be derived from the word *caro*, a "technical verb denoting the operation of cleaning wool from its impurities," though there's no origin offered for this meaning. In Henry Lyte's description of the teasel or Fuller's thistle, a plant that closely resembles the common thistle, he describes its "prickles" as being used by cloth workers to "serve their purposes," that is, helping to comb or pick out dirt and impurities from the cloth or to help raise the nap.

In the Victorian era, thistles were often included in wild gardens and pleasure grounds. They were considered stately and ornamental, and widely incorporated as a foliage plant. Today, thistles continue to appear in cottage- or wildflower-style gardens as well as country-themed wedding bouquets.

When on the breath of Autumn's breeze,
From pastures dry and brown,
Goes floating, like an idle thought,
The fair, white thistle-down;
O, then what joy to walk at will,
Upon the golden harvest-hill.

—MARY HOWITT
"Corn-Fields," *Mary Howitt's Story Book*, 1850

THISTLE FIT FOR A QUEEN

Perhaps the two most significant dresses worn by Queen Elizabeth II are her wedding (1947) and coronation (1952) gowns, both designed by Sir Norman Hartnell M.V.O. (1901–1979), Dressmaker by Appointment to the Queen and Her Majesty Queen Elizabeth the Queen Mother. The wedding dress featured silver embroidery and white seed pearl designs of traditional symbols of love and fertility such as roses, jasmine, and wheat. The coronation dress featured gold, silver, and multicolored silk embroidery of emblems representing each of the four countries within the United Kingdom as well as the states within the Commonwealth of Nations. The Tudor rose represented England; the thistle, Scotland; the leek, Wales; and a shamrock, Ireland. The thistle, according to Hartnell's book *Silver and Gold* (1955), was "embroidered in pale mauve silk and amethysts. The calyx was embroidered in reseda green silk, silver thread, and diamond dew drops." It took eight months, three dressmakers, and six embroideresses to research and complete the coronation gown. Hartnell is acknowledged by fashion historians for creating a definitive British royal style that still exists today.

TULIP

Tulipa

Declaration of love

• ◊ • ◊ •◊• ◊ •

The spring-blooimg tulip, a plant of the lily (Liliaceae) family, is primarily native to the Pamir-Alay and Tian Shan Mountains in Central Asia, also known as the Roof of the World, the English translation from the Persian name, *bam-i-dunia*, and the Celestial Mountains, respectively. These names were given for their high altitudes and the fact that they are the meeting point of some of the world's highest mountain ranges: the Himalayas with the Tian Shan, Karakoram, Kunlun, Hindu Kush, Suleman, and Hindu Raj.

The tulip is a hardy plant that does well in rough terrain and mountainous areas. Over the centuries, wild tulips have spread from these mountains, some naturally and some taken by nomadic travelers. Their natural range encompasses areas in the southern part of Ukraine, parts of Russia, the shores of the Levant in the eastern Mediterranean, Turkey, the eastern shore of the Caspian Sea, Turkmenistan through the Tian Shan, and into parts of the western Himalayas, southern Siberia, and northern China. There have also been wild tulips identified in Greece and other parts of the Balkans.

The name *tulip* has its roots in the Latin word *tulipa*, which comes from the Turkish word *tülbend*, which comes from the Persian word *dulband*, meaning "turban," "gauze," or "muslin," but was given for the flower's resemblance to a turban. According to historian Mike Dash, in his book *Tulipomania*, tulips were first "cultivated" in Persia sometime around AD 1050 in traditional walled gardens, called *pairi-daēza*, an ancient Iranian and Persian term for what is now known to mean "paradise garden."

During the later years of the Ottoman Empire, tulip gardening flourished. Tulips became an important element of tiles, pottery, textiles, art, and poetry. In fact, tulips had become such a large part of Ottoman culture that, by the sixteenth century, almost all design—including architecture, home décor, and clothing—incorporated its likeness in one way or another. Around 1717, it became a national symbol of the Ottoman Empire. According to the *Botanical Journal of the Linnaean Society*, historians refer to this twelve-year period (1718–1730) as the tulip era.

An old Persian legend that has been passed down for generations tells of the origin of the tulip and the doomed romance of two lovers in the sixth-century. Khosrow, a Persian prince, falls in love with Shirin, the princess of Armenia. Throughout their young relationship, a series of fateful events intervenes, keeping them apart for long periods of time. During these periods of separation, a humble sculptor named Farhad also falls in love with Shirin and plans to marry her. To eliminate the competition for Shirin's love, Khosrow exiles Farhad to Behistun Mountain, where he instructs him to complete what he believes will be the impossible task of carving stairs into the cliffs. While at the mountain, Farhad receives the false news that Shirin has died and flings himself from the mountain in despair. In one version of the story it is Farhad's drops of blood on the ground from which red tulips sprang. In another version, Shirin goes to the mountain looking for Farhad and, upon seeing his body, she takes her own life to be with him. Red tulips grow from the spot where their bodies lay. In yet another version, it is Khosrow who kills himself after receiving the false news of Shirin's death, and from whose blood the tulips sprang. In Henry Phillips's *Floral Emblems*, he writes that the tulip has signified the means by which a young Persian makes a declaration of love "from time immemorial," which is likely due to this story.

It's unknown exactly how the tulip arrived in Europe, but most accounts generally agree that the flower was first imported from Istanbul sometime during the middle of the sixteenth century. It's known that the first tulip to bloom in Europe was in the garden of Johann Heinrich Herwart in Augsburg, Bavaria, in 1559, as recorded by the Swiss botanist, Conrad Gesner. After the tulip's introduction, the bulbs were gradually spread throughout Austria, Germany, Italy, France, England, and the Netherlands. Holland's proximity to the coast and its sandy soil provided a particularly hospitable environment for tulips.

Many well-known botanists were responsible for creating new varieties of tulips. Among them were the English botanist James Garret (d. 1610) and his friend, fellow botanist, and author John Gerrard (c. 1545–1612), although neither of these men was as influential in the development of the tulip and its trade as the well-known French botanist Carolus Clusius (1526–1609).

Although highly regarded for his achievements in other scientific areas of botany, Clusius is primarily known for his study of tulips. Sometimes referred to as the Father of Tulips, he played a large role in the development of the Dutch tulip-trading industry while working as a professor at the University of Leiden in South Holland during the 1570s. Not only was he one of the first botanists to meticulously catalog and classify tulips, which helped merchants and traders assign prices and values, but he also frequently shipped tulip bulb samples to his colleagues in other countries, which helped to further establish tulips in gardens around Europe.

Clusius was also the first botanist to observe and define what is known as the tulip-breaking virus. The virus causes variegated coloring, weakness of the bulbs, and eventual death of the genetic line. In 1585, after almost a decade of conducting systematic studies with multicolored tulips, he concluded that the occurrences were the work of a virus. Not only was this one of the first known virus-induced plant diseases, but it also inspired the cultivation of new and rare species. Soon after this discovery, botanists learned to graft healthy bulbs onto the "broken" ones, which led to the development of countless other cultivars in even wider varieties of color and patterning. These highly coveted bulbs were the spark that lit the fire of tulipomania.

By 1600, tulips were firmly established in the world of European horticulture, largely due to Clusius's work. Many of his tulip bulbs had also been stolen from his garden over the years and distributed among the gardens of wealthy plant collectors. French aristocrats were particularly fond of the tulip, considering it a rare and novel flower with a subtle elegance that rivaled the rose. Wealthy French nobleman began giving it as a gift to women they were courting, competing with one another as to who could give a more rare or valuable tulip. Soon, Parisian noblewomen were using these gifts to decorate their cleavages and dresses. As Paris was, and still is, extremely influential in the world of fashion and trends, the rest of Europe followed suit.

Although tulips were more widely available in Europe in the early seventeenth century, they were still considered a somewhat rare and expensive luxury item. The selective breeding process for fancier varieties was slow and imprecise, and prices for these bulbs only continued to climb. In the early 1620s, the Semper Augustus tulip appeared in the Dutch Republic. It was a red-and-white flame-streaked flower that was considered the most beautiful and rarest of all tulips. A bulb-hunting frenzy ensued, with Dutch connoisseurs eager to find more of these rare bulbs, or those of a tulip that could possibly eclipse its beauty—and tulipomania began. Tulips quickly become a major export for Holland and, by the mid-1630s, a speculative market based on tulip futures had emerged. Rare bulbs were going for thousands of florins and people began to trade their possessions, houses, and lands for the flowers, thinking them a safe bet to acquire even greater wealth through selling them.

As with most highly lucrative financial bubbles, tulipomania lasted only a year. The tulip market collapsed suddenly in February 1637. One contributing factor was the newly grafted cultivars that had flooded the market. This led to many buyers and few sellers. A second factor was an outbreak of the bubonic plague, which simultaneously increased risk-taking behaviors in some people, who paid outrageous prices for tulips they would never be able to resell at a profit. This also scared healthy people away from attending bulb auctions or following through on bulb deliveries. The collapse left many people, including the famous Dutch landscape painter Jan van Goyen, in serious financial ruin. Although prices and enthusiasm for tulips had been significantly tempered by the end of the craze, they remained a top export of the Netherlands, which remains to this day the world's leading supplier of commercial tulips, producing two billion tulips per year. About 77 percent of the world's flower bulbs come from this region, with 90 percent of tulips originating there.

In *Flora's Dictionary*, Elizabeth Washington Wirt writes that the tulip had always been considered a rival to the rose because it displayed "a more gorgeous and varied tinting of colors, to balance the superior fragrance of her compeer." This may be why, despite their presence in gardens and exhibitions, Victorian gardeners were very divided on its beauty and value. Because of this, the tulip was not nearly as popular in England as it was in other parts of Europe.

Today visiting tulip gardens is popular worldwide, with travelers often making their way to the large gardens of the Netherlands, Turkey, and even England for annual tulip celebrations. One of the oldest florists' societies in the world, Wakefield & North of England Tulip Society, founded in 1836, is based in North Yorkshire. It is the only remaining society specializing in tulips and hosts annual events. During the English Tulip Festival, a recommended stop is the Pashley Manor Gardens in East Sussex, which, according to *Smithsonian* magazine, contains more than twenty-five thousand tulips.

THE AUDREY HEPBURN TULIP

The actress Audrey Hepburn was of Dutch descent and was known to have not only a love of gardening, but also a special fondness for tulips. Her mother had been a Dutch noblewoman from Arnhem, a city in the eastern Netherlands. Her family traveled frequently when she was younger and, in an attempt to take refuge in a neutral country at the start of World War II, they relocated from England to Arnhem. Unfortunately, the Nazis came to occupy the Netherlands for five years, during which time food was incredibly scarce. According to the book *Audrey at Home: Memories of My Mother's Kitchen*, written by Hepburn's son Luca Dotti, his mother's family relied on boiled grass and tulip bulbs to avoid starving to death. Dotti says the white tulip was Hepburn's favorite flower and that in 1990, a snowy white tulip hybrid developed in Holland by Ivan der Mark was named for her in honor of her memorable career and charitable work with UNICEF. According to Dotti, during the tulip dedication ceremony Hepburn said the naming of this flower in her honor was the single most romantic thing to happen to her in her life.

◦ ◊ ◦ ◊ ◦ ◊ ◦ ◊ ◦

Like tulip-beds of different shape and dyes,
Bending beneath the invisible west-wind's sighs.

—THOMAS MOORE
"The Veiled Prophet of Khorassan," *Lalla-Rookh*, 1817

VIOLET

Viola odorata

Modesty

• ◇ • ◇ •◇• ◇ •

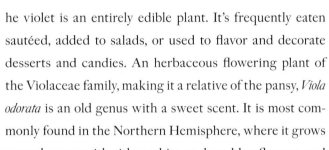

The violet is an entirely edible plant. It's frequently eaten sautéed, added to salads, or used to flavor and decorate desserts and candies. An herbaceous flowering plant of the Violaceae family, making it a relative of the pansy, *Viola odorata* is an old genus with a sweet scent. It is most commonly found in the Northern Hemisphere, where it grows wild as creeping ground cover, with either white or deep-blue flowers, and heart-shaped leaves.

The violet's beautiful coloring and enjoyable fragrance made it a welcome cultivar in the Victorian garden. Its lack of showiness and small stature, combined with these delightful qualities, contributed to its assignment as a symbol of modesty. In *Floral Emblems*, Henry Phillips wrote that the violet was an unobtrusive flower "no less honored by its emblem than the rose or myrtle," and a necessary complement to enhance "the delights [those plants] can inspire." In *Flora's Dictionary*, Elizabeth Washington Wirt notes that some etymologists had traced the name of the flower to Ia, a daughter of Midas, who was turned into a violet by the goddess Diana in order to hide her from the god Apollo. She writes that the flower has a "beautiful modest blossom that still retains the bashful timidity of the nymph." She even goes on to mention that "the poetry, the romance, the scenery of every country, is embroidered with *violets*."

In *Flora's Dictionary*, Wirt also briefly mentions another Greek myth in which the violet plays a role: the story of Io, the mortal lover of Zeus who was turned into a white heifer. *A niewe Herball* interprets this myth in further detail, explaining that the sweet violet was called *ion* in Greek, after Io, a maiden that the god Zeus had loved. Because Io was carrying Zeus's child, he turned her into a heifer, or "gallant cowe," so that she would be hidden from his jealous wife, the goddess Hera. Zeus loved Io. In her honor, he commanded the earth to bring forth violets so that she could have something "more delicate and holsome" to eat. He called this flower *ion*.

In addition to having a strong appreciation for any flower that might have a myth or lore attached to it, the Victorians welcomed plants that could be used medicinally. In *A niewe Herball*, Henry Lyte wrote that a decoction, or syrup, of violets could be used to treat fevers or inflammation of the liver, lungs, and breasts, as well as help relieve coughs and sore throats, especially in young children. He also wrote that a paste of pounded violets with oil could be laid upon the head to help with headaches and to remove the heat of a fever. It could also be used as a sleeping aid and to generally prevent "dulnesse or heavinesse of Spirite." Last, he suggested that, when the seed of violets was taken with wine or water, it could be useful against the sting of a scorpion.

In T. F. Dyer's *The Folklore of Plants*, he informs the Victorian reader that the violet, along with roses, anemone, thyme, melilot, hyacinth, crocus, and yellow lily, was often used in Greek ceremonial garlands and chaplets. He also writes that, although bridal bouquets had initially been comprised of rare and costly flowers, bouquets of "country flowers" had become more popular over the years and, because of this, violets and primroses were always in demand in the springtime. Today, violets are used in any garden or bouquet that is striving for a vintage or country-garden theme.

ROSES ARE RED, VIOLETS ARE BLUE

The children's rhyme "Roses are red/Violets are blue/Sugar is sweet/And so are you" has its roots in Edmund Spenser's *The Faerie Queene* (1596). Spanning six books, Spenser's epic poem follows the adventures of six medieval knights, each of whom represents a different virtue of the Elizabethan era: holiness (Book I), temperance (Book II), chastity (Book III), friendship (Book IV), justice (Book V), and courtesy (Book VI). In each book, the knight at the center of the narrative is faced with a challenge that affects the virtue he represents. In this excerpt from the beginning of Book III, an unknown third-person narrator, who praises the virtue of chastity before beginning the unique story of Knight Britomart. In it, the narrator describes how the virgin huntress Belphoebe was conceived by her chaste and virtuous mother Chrysogonee:

> *It was upon a Sommers shinie day,*
> *When Titan faire his beames did display,*
> *In a fresh fountaine, far from all mens vew,*
> *She bath'd her brest the boyling heat t'allay;*
> *She bath'd with roses red and violets blew,*
> *And all the sweetest flowers that in the forrest grew.*
>
> *Till faint through yrksome weariness, adowne*
> *Upon the grassy ground her selfe she layd*
> *To sleepe, the whiles a gentle slombring swowne*
> *Upon her fell, all naked bare displayd;*
> *The sunbeams bright upon her body playd.*
>
> *Being through former bathing mollifide,*
> *And pierst into her wombe, where they embayd*
> *With so sweet sence and secret power unspide,*
> *That in her pregnant flesh they shortly fructifide.*

Because Chrysogonee had been impregnated by sunbeams and remained untouched by man, Belphoebe came to exemplify chastity and virginity. Spenser intended to write twelve books for this poem, but only partially completed the seventh, which was meant to represent constancy.

ZINNIA

Zinnia

Absence

• ◇ • ◇ • ◇ • ◇ •

he zinnia is one of the many flowers cultivated by the Aztecs, a fact noted by Spanish hidalgos during their conquest of Mexico in the 1520s. A flowering shrub of the daisy family (Asteraceae) that primarily grows in dry grasslands, it's native to North, Central, and South America. The Spanish viewed the zinnia as a weedy and unattractive plant, referring to it as *mal de ojos*, meaning "evil eyes," and chose not to bring it back to Europe. Because of this, zinnia seeds didn't arrive in Europe until the early 1700s and were largely ignored until the 1800s, when Victorian gardening was thriving.

According to Scottish botanist Philip Miller's *Gardener's and Botanist's Dictionary* (1807), zinnia seeds were first brought directly from Peru to The Royal Garden at Paris by an unnamed source sometime before 1753. That was the year Miller, who was head gardener at the Chelsea Physic Garden in London, first received his own seeds from Paris. The following summer, he successfully produced the first flowering zinnias in England. Botanists continued selectively cultivating zinnias and, in 1796, Casimiro Gomez Ortega, director of the Royal Gardens of Madrid, had produced a viable seed from a purple variety of *Zinnia elegans*, a variety known to produce larger-than-usual flower heads, which he then sent to England. From there, curiosity about the zinnia spread among European gardeners, which led to the development of a scarlet *Zinnia elegans* in 1829, then finally the double-flowered cultivar in 1858.

Carl Linnaeus named the zinnia in honor of the German anatomist and botanist, Johann Gottfried Zinn, who had been the head of the botanic garden at University of Göttingen from 1753 until his death in 1759. Zinn is known for giving one of the first and most detailed descriptions of the anatomy of the human eye, in addition to his botanical studies in Mexico.

Zinnias are hardy and easy-to-grow plants that can be hybridized with little difficulty, which helped them to gain popularity among Victorians. The 1874 issue of *The Gardener's Chronicle* described them as "vibrant" and "dazzling" flowers, growing with four-inch-wide blooms in "shades of crimson, scarlet, magenta, pink, orange, primrose, and white" at the Brayfield Gardens in Buckinghamshire. The magazine also enthusiastically noted that zinnias were well adapted to planting in isolated flower beds and could grow rapidly.

It's unclear why zinnias were made the emblem of absence, as they were welcome in the Victorian garden. Today, zinnias continue to be enjoyed for their ease of cultivation, bright colors, and ability to attract butterflies and other pollinators. They're also frequently used in seasonal bouquets and decorations for weddings and parties that call for a rustic theme, especially in the autumn.

• ◇ • ◇ • ◇• ◇ •

Absence diminishes little passions and increases great ones,
as the wind extinguishes candles and fans a fire.

—FRANÇOIS DE LA ROCHEFOUCAULD
Reflections; or Sentences and Moral Maxims, 1665

Zinnia Notes

While red lettuce was the first "flowering" plant to sprout in space in June 2014, the zinnia was the first real flower to grow and bloom there. According to NASA, the growth of zinnia plants was activated on November 16, 2015, as part of a Vegetable Production System (VEGGIE) experiment; the first blooms were photographed on January 16, 2016. The experiment aims to help scientists learn sustainable food-production and crop-growing techniques as they explore Mars and embark on other deep space exploration missions.

• ◊ •

Native Americans once used zinnias as a source for yellow dye to decorate tools, clothing, and the body.

• ◊ •

The Navajo people had a legend that the yellow zinnia was sent by a Mother Nature deity to help lead a Navajo child named Straight Arrow in his search to find a way to prevent the destruction of their crops. It is believed that this is why the Navajo would plant yellow zinnias with their corn.

INDEX OF FLOWERS AND THEIR MEANINGS

• ◇ • ◇ • ◇ • ◇ •

There has always been some variation among floriography dictionaries regarding their choice of meaning for flowers; a standard was never established. The symbolism in this book was chosen either for its prevalence, the historical evidence supporting it, or both. For more on the assignment of meaning refer to the Introduction to this book.

Acknowledgments

• ◇ • ◇ • ◇ • ◇ •

My editor, Elizabeth Sullivan, is the best editor in the world. If there are any Best Editor in the World mugs out there, they should have a little footnote saying, "*We're talking about Liz." This book wouldn't exist without her guidance, openness, and encouragement. It means a lot to know that, when you're really investing yourself in a project like this, the people you're working with are right there with you, staying just as invested in the outcome. She's smart, kind, and lovely to work with. I really can't say enough nice things about her as well as the team at Harper Design.

During the year in which I wrote and illustrated this book, I have lived and breathed it and, for the most part, loved it. But there were certainly days when I needed extra moral support or guidance with writing and research, or feedback on my illustration ideas. I couldn't have done this project without my husband, Jordan, his family, and my agent, Fran Black. They've been my biggest cheerleaders, always ready to brainstorm concepts for illustrations or help me find the right wording when I felt stuck. They offered to help with research—and did—when my brain felt like quitting, and they reminded me almost daily that I was doing a great job.

Finally, my dog, Archie, lent his constant services for stress-relieving games of fetch, soft head pats, and doggy kisses—and those are just irreplaceable.

I love you all.

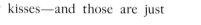

SELECT BIBLIOGRAPHY

Books

Aesop's Fables. New York: Samuel R. Wells, 1868.

Aubrey, John. *Memoires of Natural Remarques in the County of Wilts.* London: Middle Hill Press, 1838.

Bailey, L. H. *The Standard Cyclopedia of Horticulture: Vol. II.* New York: The Macmillan Company, 1914.

Beals, Katharine M. *Flower Lore and Legend.* New York: Henry Holt and Company, 1917.

Berens, E. M. *Myths and Legends of Ancient Greece and Rome.* Project Gutenberg, 2007.

Boyle, Frederick. *About Orchids; A Chat.* London: Chapman and Hall, 1893.

Brotherston, R. P. *The Book of Cut Flowers: A Complete Guide to the Preparing, Arranging, and Preserving of Flowers for Decorative Purposes.* Edinburgh: T.N. Foulis, 1906.

Burney, Frances. *Evelina, or, The History of a Young Lady's Entrance into the World.* London: J. M. Dent and Company, 1778.

Byron, Lord. *The Corsair, a Tale.* London: Thomas Davison, Whitefriars, 1814.

California Arboretum Foundation. *Lasca Leaves.* Arcadia: California Arboretum Foundation, 1950.

Campbell, John Gregorson. *Superstitions of the Highlands & Islands of Scotland.* Glasgow: J. MacLehose and Sons, 1900.

Carter, Anthony John. "Myths and Mandrakes." *Journal of the Royal Society of Medicine* 96, no. 3 (2003): 144-147.

Carter, William C. *Marcel Proust: A Life.* New Haven: Yale University Press, 2013.

Chamberlain, Basil Hall. *The Classical Poetry of the Japanese.* London: Trübner, 1880.

Chambers, R. *The Book of Days: A Miscellany.* London: W. and R. Chambers, 1864.

Chan, Benjamin, Sarah Viner, Mike Parker Pearson, Umberto Albarella, and Rob Ixer. "Resourcing Stonehenge: Patterns of Human, Animal and Goods Mobility in the Late Neolithic." In *Moving on in Neolithic Studies*, edited by Jim Leary and Thomas Kador, 28-44. Oxford: Oxbow Books, 2016.

Chapman, George. *All Fools.* London: Thomas Thorpe, 1605.

Coitir, Niall Mac. *Irish Wild Plants: Myths, Legends, and Folklore.* Cork, Ireland: The Collins Press, 2006.

Culpeper, Nicholas. *The Complete Herbal.* London: Foulsham, 1843.

Cumo, Christopher. *Encyclopedia of Cultivated Plants: From Acacia to Zinnia.* Santa Barbara: ABC-CLIO, 2013.

Daniels, Cora Lin and C. M. Stevans. *Encyclopedia of Superstitions, Folklore, and the Occult Sciences of the World.* Chicago: J. H. Yewdale and Sons, 1903.

Darwin, Charles. *The Various Contrivances by Which Orchids Are Fertilised by Insects.* London: John Murray, 1890.

Dash, Mike. *Tulipomania.* New York: Three Rivers Press, 1999.

Dean, Richard. *The Sweet Pea Bicentenary Celebration.* Ealing: Richard Dean, 1900.

Dunglison, Robley. *Medical Lexicon: A Dictionary of Medical Science*, 6th Ed. Philadelphia: Lea and Blanchard, 1846.

Dyer, T. F. Thiselton. *The Folklore of Plants.* London: Chatto and Windus, 1889.

Egmond, Florike. *The Exotic World of Carolus Clusius (1526-1609).* Leiden: Leiden University Library, 2009.

Faust, Miklos. "Origin and Dissemination of Cherry." In *Horticultural Reviews: Volume 19,* edited by Jules Janick, 263–318. New York: John Wiley & Sons, Incorporated, 1997.

Fell, Derek. *Secrets of Monet's Garden: Bringing the Beauty of Monet's Style to Your Own Garden.* New York: Friedman/Fairfax Publishers, 1997.

Ferguson, Donita. *Fun with Flowers: How to Arrange Yourself and Your Flowers.* Boston: Houghton Mifflin, 1939.

Fisher, Celia. *Flowers in Medieval Manuscripts.* Toronto: University of Toronto Press, 2004.

Folkard, Richard. *Plant Lore, Legends, and Lyrics.* London: S. Low, Marston, Searle, and Rivington, 1884.

Friend, Hilderic. *Flowers and Flower Lore.* London: S. Sonneschein, Le Bas, and Lowrey, 1886.

Gerarde, John. *The Herball, or, Generall Historie of Plantes.* Toronto: Thomas Fisher, 1638.

Giles, Herbert A. *Gems of Chinese Literature.* Shanghai: Kelly and Balsh, Limited, 1922.

Godwin, Harry. *The History of the British Flora: A Factual Basis for Phytogeography.* London: Cambridge University Press, 1956.

Goldthorpe, Caroline. *From Queen to Empress: Victorian Dress, 1837–1877*. New York: The Metropolitan Museum of Art, 1989.

Hassard, Annie. *Floral Decorations for the Dwelling House: A Practical Guide to the Home Arrangement of Plants and Flowers*. London: Macmillan and Company, 1875.

Holinshed, Raphael. *The Chronicles of England, Irelande, and Scotlande*. 1585.

Holley, Dennis. *General Biology II: Organisms and Ecology*. Indianapolis: Dog Ear Publishing, 2017.

Hooper, E. J., Thomas Affleck, Charles Foster, and Charles W. Elliott. *The Western Farmer and Gardener*. Cincinnati: J.A. and U.P. James, 1850.

Hottes, Alfred Carl. *A Little Book of Annuals*. New York: The A. T. De La Mare Company, Incorporated, 1922.

Howard, Michael. *Traditional Folk Remedies: A Comprehensive Herbal*. Century: 1987.

Huish, Marcus Bourne. *Japan and Its Art*. London: B. T. Batsford, 1912.

Hunt, Robert, *Popular Romances of the West of England; or, The Drolls, Traditions, and Superstitions of Old Cornwall* (London: John Camden Hotten, 1871), pp. 384–385.

Ives, Colta Feller. *The Great Wave: The Influence of Japanese Woodcuts on French Prints*. New York: The Metropolitan Museum of Art, 1974.

Jameson, Eric. *The Natural History of Quackery*. Illinois: Charles C. Thomas, 1961.

Johnson, Cleatrice. *Mizue Sawano: The Art of the Cherry Tree*. Brooklyn: The Brooklyn Botanical Garden, 2006.

Johnson, George William. *The Dahlia: Its Culture, Uses, and History*. London: Simpkin, Marshall and Company, 1847.

Johnston, Ruth A. *All Things Medieval: An Encyclopedia of the Medieval World*. Santa Barbara: Greenwood, 2011.

K'Eogh. *Botanalogia Universalis Hibernica*. George Harrison, 1735.

Kantor, Helene J. *Plant Ornament: Its Origin and Development in the Ancient Near East*. Chicago: The University of Chicago, 1945.

Karr, Alphonse. *Lettres Écrites de Mon Jardin*. Paris: Michel Lévy Fréres, 1855.

Kaya, Yalcin, Igor Balalic, and Vladimir Milic. "Eastern Europe Perspectives on Sunflower Production and Processing." In *Sunflower Chemistry, Production, Processing and Utilization*, edited by Enrique Martínez Force, 575-638. Illinois: AOCS Press, 2015.

Kingsbury, Noel. *Garden Flora: The Natural and Cultural History of the Plants in Your Garden*. Timber Press, 2016.

Král, Martin. *Of Dahlia Myths and Aztec Mythology*. Seattle: The Puget Sound Dahlia Association, 2014.

Laughlin, Clara Elizabeth. *The Complete Hostess*. New York: D. Appleton and Company, 1906.

Liddell, Henry George and Robert Scott. *A Greek-English Lexicon Revised and Augmented throughout by Sir Henry Stuart Jones with the Assistance of Roderick McKenzie*. Oxford: Clarendon Press, 1940.

Lim, T.K. *Edible Medicinal and Non-Medical Plants: Volume 11*. New York: Springer International Publishing Switzerland, 2016.

von Linne, Carl. *Species Plantarum*. Holmiae: Impensis Laurentii Salvii, 1753.

Loudon, John Claudius. *An Encyclopædia of Gardening*. London: Longman, Green, Longman, and Roberts, 1860.

———. *Arboretum Et Fruticetum Britannicum*. London: Longman, Orme, Brown, Green, and Longman, 1838.

Lyte, Henry. *A Niewe Herball*. London: Gerard Dewes, 1578.

H. Goodyear. *The Grammar of the Lotus*. London: Sampson, Low, Marston and Company, 1891.

Martyn, Thomas. *The Gardener's and Botanist's Dictionary*. London: 1807.

McKevley, Susan Delano. *The Lilac*. New York: The Macmillan Company, 1928.

Merriman, Effie Woodward. *Socials*. Chicago: C.H. Sergel and Company, 1891.

Molyneux, Edwin. *Chrysanthemums and Their Culture*. London, 1898.

Montagu, Lady M. W. *The Letters of Lady M. W. Montagu*. Paris: Raudry's European Library, 1840.

Moore, N. Hudson. *Tulips, Daffodils, and Crocuses*. New York: Stokes, 1904.

Moore, Thomas. *The Poetical Works of Thomas Moore*. Paris: A. and W. Galignani, 1827.

Murrat, Margaret Alice. *The Witch-Cult in Western Europe*. Oxford: Clarendon Press, 1921.

Ono, Ayako. *Japonisme in Britain*. London: Routledge Curzon, 2003.

Parsons, Samuel Bowne. *Parsons on the Rose*. New York: Orange Judd, 1908.

Pettigrew, Thomas Joseph. *A History of Egyptian Mummies*. London: Longman, Rees, Orme, Brown, Green, and Longman, 1834.

Phillips, Henry. *Floral Emblems*. London: Saunders and Otley, 1825.

Piesse, G. W. Septimus. *The Art of Perfumery*. Philadelphia: Lisay and Blakiston, 1857.

Rees, Abraham. *The Cyclopedia or Universal Dictionary of Arts, Sciences, and Literature.* London: Longman, Hurst, Rees, Orme, and Brown, 1819.

Rhind, William. *A History of the Vegetable Kingdom: Embracing the Physiology, Classification, and Culture of Plants, with Their Various Uses to Man and the Lower Animals, and their applications in the Arts, Manufactures, and Domestic Economy.* Glasgow: Blackie and Son, 1841.

Robinson, W. *The English Flower Garden.* London: J. Murray, 1897.

Rouchardat, M. *Répertoire de Pharmacie: Recueil Pratique.* Paris: Au Bureau du Journal, 1860.

Rousseau, Jean-Jacques. *Confessions.* New York: Knopf, 1923.

Ruddock, E. Harris. *Homeopathic Vade Mecum of Modern Medicine and Surgery.* London: Jarrold and Sons, 1867.

Sanders, Jack. *The Secrets of Wildflowers: A Delightful Feast of Little-Known Facts, Folklore, and History.* Connecticut: The Lyons Press, 2003.

Sands, Robert Charles. *The Writings of Robert C. Sands, in Prose and Verse, with a Memoir of the Author in Two Volumes, Volume I.* New York: Harper & Borthers, 1834.

Seaton, Beverly. *The Language of Flowers: A History.* Charlottesville: The University Press of Virginia, 1995.

Shelley, Percy Bysshe. *The Sensitive Plant.* London: Heinemann, 1820.

The Gardeners' Chronicle. London: 1841.

The Gardeners' Magazine. London: Gardeners' Magazine Office, 1860.

Thorpe, Benjamin. *Northern Mythology, Comprising the Principal Popular Traditions of Scandinavia, North Germany, and the Netherlands.* London: Edward Lumley, 1853.

Thomas, H. H. *Sweet Peas and How to Grow Them.* London: Cassell and Company, 1909.

Turner, Elizabeth Hutton. *Georgia O'Keeffe: The Poetry of Things.* Washington D.C.: The Phillips Collection, 1999.

Valentine, Laura. *Beautiful Bouquets, Culled from the Poets of All Countries.* London: F. Warne and Company, 1869.

Webb, Jessica. *What Lies Beneath: Orthodoxy and the Occult in Victorian Literature.* Cardiff: Cardiff University, 2010.

Wilder, Louise Beebe. *The Fragrant Path: A Book About Sweet Scented Flowers and Leaves.* Washington: Point Roberts, 1932.

Wirt, Elizabeth Washington. *Flora's Dictionary.* Baltimore: Lucas Brothers, 1855.

Wolverton, B.C., Anne Johnson, and Keith Bounds. *Interior Landscape Plants for Indoor Air Pollution Abatement.* Mississippi: National Aeronautics Space Center, 1989.

Wood, George B. and Franklin Bache. *The Dispensatory of the United States of America.* Philadelphia: J. B. Lippincott and Company, 1858.

Periodicals

Arora, D., A. Rani, and A. Sharma. "A Review on Phytochemistry and Ethnopharmacological Aspects of Genus *Calendula*." *Pharmacognosy Review* 7, no. 14 (2013): 179–187.

Atamian, H. S., N. M. Creux, E. A. Brown, et al. "Circadian Regulation of Sunflower Heliotropism, Floral Orientation, and Pollinator Visits." *Science* 353, no. 6299 (2016): 587–590.

Bellincampi, Suzan. "All About Azaleas, from A to Z." *Martha's Vineyard Magazine.* April 27, 2016.

Berdai, M. A., S. Labib, K. Chetouani, and M.Harandou. "Atropa Belladonna Intoxication: A Case Report." *Pan African Medical Journal* 11 (2012): 72.

Blumer, D. "The Illness of Vincent van Gogh." *American Journal of Photography* 159, no. 4 (2002): 519–526.

Brennand, Mark, Maisie Taylor, Trevor Ashwin, et al. "The Survey and Excavation of a Bronze Age Timber Circle at Holme-next-the-Sea, Norfolk, 1998-9." *Proceedings of the Prehistoric Society* 69 (2003): 1–84.

Castro, P., J. L. Miranda, P. Gomez, D. M. Escalante, F. L. Segura, A. Martin, F. Fuentes, A. Blanco, J.M. Ordovas, F. P. and Jimenez. "Comparison of an Oleic Acid Enriched–Diet vs NCEP-I Diet on LDL Susceptibility to Oxidative Modifications." *European Journal of Clinical Nutrition* 54, no.1 (2000): 61–67.

Christenhusz, Maarten, Rafaël Govaerts, John C. David, et al. "Tiptoe through the Tulips—Cultural History, Molecular Phylogenetics and Classification of *Tulipa* (Liliaceae)." *Botanical Journal of the Linnean Society* 172, no. 3 (2013): 280–283

Clute, W. N. "Plant Names and Their Meanings—IX Leguminosae—I." *The American Botanist* 1, no. 27 (1921): 129–134.

Chang, C. W., M. T. Lin, S. S. Lee, et al. "Differential Inhibition of Reverse Transcriptase and Cellular DNA Polymerase-alpha Activities by Lignans Isolated from Chinese Herbs, Phyllanthus Myrtifolius Moon, and Tannins from Lonicera Japonica Thunb and Castanopsis Hystrix." *MEDLINE* 27, no. 4 (1995): 367–374.

Declair, V. "The Usefulness of Topical Application of Essential Fatty Acids (EFA) to Prevent Pressure Ulcers." *Ostomy Wound Management* 43, no. 5 (1997): 48–54.

Dobkin de Rios, M. "The Influence of Psychotropic Flora and Fauna on Maya Religion." *Current Anthropology* 15, no. 2 (1974): 147–164.

Edwards, K. "Rediscovering Slave Burial Sites." *Genealogy Insider*, October/November 2013, 6–7.

Elliott, B. "Flower Shows in Nineteenth-Century England." *Garden History* 29, no. 2 (2001): 171–184.

Franklin, J. J. "The Life of the Buddha in Victorian England." *ELH* 72, no. 4 (2005): 941–974.

Gao, Y.-D., A. J. Harris, and X.-J. He. "Morphological and Ecological Divergence of Lilium and Nomocharis within the Hengduan Mountains and Qinghai-Tibetan Plateau May Result from Habitat Specialization and Hybridization." *BMC Evolutionary Biology* 15 (2015): 147.

Garber, P. M. "Tulipmania." *The Journal of Political Economy* 97, no. 3 (1989): 535–560.

Guarrera, P. M. "Household Dyeing Plants and Traditional Uses in Some Areas of Italy." *Journal of Ethnobiology and Ethnomedicine* no. 2 (2006): 9.

Hanson, H. C. "Western Agricultural Exchanges." *The Florist and Agricultural Journal* 2, no. 1 (1853): 386–388.

Kandeler, R. and W. R. Ullrich. "Symbolism of Plants: Examples from European-Mediterranean Culture Presented with Biology and History of Art." *Journal of Experimental Botany* 60, no. 3 (2009): 715–717.

Kornienko, A. and A. Evidente. "Chemistry, Biology and Medicinal Potential of Narciclasine and its Congeners." *Chemical Reviews* 108, no. 6 (2008): 1982–2014.

Koulivand, P. H., M. K. Ghadiri, and A. Gorji. "Lavender and the Nervous System." *Evidence-based Complementary and Alternative Medicine* (2013).doi: 10.1155/2013/681304.

Lee, T. C. "Van Gogh's Vision, Digitalis Intoxication?" *JAMA* 245, no. 7 (1981): 727–729.

Lesnaw, J. A. and S. A. Ghabrial. "Tulip Breaking: Past, Present, and Future." *Plant Disease* 84, no. 10 (2000): 1052–1060.

Mai, D. H. "The Floral Change in the Tertiary of the Rhön Mountains (Germany)." *Acta Paleobotanica* 47, no. 1 (2007): 135–143.

Merlin, M. D. "Archaeological Evidence for the Tradition of Psychoactive Plant Use in the Old World." *Economic Botany* 57, no. 3 (2003): 295–323.

Morris, B. "Gala Night at MET Hails Saint Laurent." *New York Times*, December 1983, 10.

Mucke, H. A. M. "The Case of Galantamine: Repurposing and Late Blooming of a Cholinergic Drug." *Future Science OA* 1, no. 4 (2015): 73.

Mustoe, G. E. "Hydrangea Fossils from the Early Tertiary Chuckanut Formation." *Western Washington University* (2002).

Nagase, A. "Japanese Floriculture Development in the Edo Period (1603-1868)." *Hot Research* 65 (2011): 1–5.

Plaitakis, A., R. C. Duvoisin. "Homer's Moly Identified as Galanthus Nivalis L.: Physiologic Antidote to Stramonium Poisoning." *Journal of Clinical Pharmacology* 6, no. 1 (1983): 1–5.

"Plumier, Charles (1646-1704)," *JSTOR*. plants. jstor.org. Accessed February 25, 2019.

Streng, B., K. W. Ruprecht, and R. Wittern. "Johann Gottfried Zinn—a Franconian Anatomist and Botanist." *Klin Mondl Augenheilkd* 199, no. 1 (1991): 57–61.

The British Museum. "Chinese Symbols." *China: A Journey to the East.*

Todt, D. L. "Relic Gold: The Long Journey of the Chinese Narcissus." *Pacific Horticulture* 73, no. 1 (2012).

Van der Kooi, C. J., A. G. Dyer, and D. G. Stavenga. "Is Floral Iridescence a Biologically Relevant Cue in Plant-Pollinator Signaling?" *New Phytologist* 205, no. 1 (2015), 18-20.

Vignolini, S., E. Moyroud, T. Hingant, et al. "The Flower of Hibiscus Trionum Is both Visibly and Measurably Iridescent." *New Phytologist* 205, no. 1 (2015), 97–101.

Wei-Haas, M. "Mummy Yields Earliest Known Egyptian Embalming Recipe." *National Geographic*. August 15, 2018.

Weland, G. "The Alpha and Omega of Dahlias." *The American Dahlia Society.*

Whitley, G. R. "The Medicinal and Nutritional Properties of Dahlia SPP." *Journal of Ethnopharmacology* 14, no. 1 (1985): 75–82.

Wolf, P. "Creativity and Chronic Disease Vincent van Gogh (1853-1890)." *Western Journal of Medicine* 175, no. 5 (2001): 348.

Websites

"A Short History of Dahlia Hybridization." The Stanford Dahlia Project. http ://web.stanford.edu/group/dahlia _genetics/dahlia_history.htm. Accessed February 25, 2019.

"Acacia." Online Etymology Dictionary. https://www.etymonline.com/word/acacia. Accessed March 1, 2019.

"Academic Dress." Oxford Students. https://www.ox.ac.uk/students/academic /dress?wssl=1. Accessed February 22, 2019.

Agrella, R. A. "Brief History of Tulips." Heirloom Gardener. https://www. heirloomgardener.com/plant-profiles /ornamental/history-of-tulips -zmaz14fzsbak. Last modified Fall 2014.

"Ancient Egyptian New Kingdom Faience Rosettes – 1550 BC." http://www.artancient .com/antiquities-for-sale/cultures /egyptian-antiquities-for-sale/egyptian -new-kingdom-faience-rosettes- 1550-bc-31003.html. artancient.com. Accessed February 25, 2019.

Antolini, K. L. "The Tenacious Woman Who Helped Keep Mother's Day Alive." Smithsonian.com. https://www .smithsonianmag.com/arts-culture /tenacious-woman-who-helped-keep -mothers-day-alive-180955205/. Last modified May 8, 2015.

Arayavand, A. and B. Grami. "Lily." Encyclopaedia Iranica. http:// www.iranicaonline.org/articles/lily. Last modified September 28, 2015.

Ashliman, D. L. "The Nickert." German Changeling Legends. http://www.pitt .edu/~dash/gerchange.html#nickert. Accessed March 1, 2019.

"Azaleas." Magnolia Plantation and Gardens. https://www.magnoliaplantation.com /azaleas.html. Accessed February 22, 2019.

Basu, S. "Celebrating the Jasmine." The Hindu. https://www.thehindu.com/books /books-reviews/Celebrating-the-jasmine /article12399523.ece. Last modified October 18, 2016.

"Bellis Perennis." Flora of North America. http://www.efloras.org/florataxon. aspx?flora_id=1&taxon_id=200023530. Accessed February 25, 2019.

Bender, S. "Azalea: Essential Southern Plant." Southern Living. https://www .southernliving.com/home-garden/gardens /azalea-plants. Accessed February 22, 2019.

———. "A Brief History of the Azalea." Southern Living. https://www.southernliving.com /home-garden/gardens/southern-gardening -azalea-history. Accessed February 22, 2019.

"Bittersweet Nightshade." The Ohio State University. https://www.oardc.ohio-state .edu/weedguide/single_weed.php?id=82. Accessed February 28, 2019.

"Bush Morning-Glory." United States Department of Agriculture.https://plants .usda.gov/plantguide/pdf/pg_iple.pdf? ref=organicgglunkwn&prid=pfseog -glunkwn. Accessed February 28, 2019.

Butler, M. L. "Mărțișor: The Romanian Allegory of Life and Death Is a Lucky Charm." HuffPost. hhttps://www.huffpost .com/entry/m%C4%83r%C8%9Bi%C8%99or -the-romanian-allegory-of-life-and-death -is_b_58b56936e4b0e5fdf61976ab. Last modified February 28, 2017.

"Buttercup." United States Department of Agriculture Forest Service Nez Perce National Historic Trail. fhttps://www .fs.usda.gov/detail/npnht/learningcenter /kids/?cid=fsbdev3_055755. Accessed February 22, 2019.

Cahill, B. "A Rose by Any Other Name? Call It an Herb." The Denver Post. https://www .denverpost.com/2012/05/09/a-rose-by-any -other-name-call-it-an-herb/. Last modified May 1, 2016.

"Calendula." Georgetown University Medical Center. https://sites.google.com/a /georgetown.edu/urban-herbs/calendula. Accessed February 28, 2019.

"Calendula Officinalis." Missouri Botanical Garden. http://www.missouribotanicalgarden .org/PlantFinder/PlantFinderDetails .aspx?taxonid=277409&isprofile=0&. Accessed February 28, 2019.

"Carnation." Dictionary.com. https://www .dictionary.com/browse/carnation. Accessed February 22, 2019.

Charles, D. "How the Russians Saved America's Sunflower." NPR. https://www.npr.org /sections/thesalt/2012/01/05/144695733/how -the-russians-saved-americas-sunflower. Last modified January 5, 2012.

Chinou, I. "Assessment Report on Rosa Gallica L., Rosa Centifolia L., Rosa Damascena Mill., Flos." European Medicines Agency. https:// www.ema.europa.eu/en/documents/herbal -report/draft-assessment-report-rosa-centifolia -l-rosa-gallica-l-rosa-damascena-mill-flos_ en.pdf. Last modified December 15, 2013.

"Crosscurrents: Modern Art from the Sam Rose and Julie Walters Collection: Hibiscus with Plumeria." Smithsonian American Art Museum Renwick Gallery. https://americanart.si.edu/artwork/hibiscus-plumeria-73942. Accessed February 26, 2019.

Stradley, L. "Culinary Lavender." What's Cooking America. https://whatscookingamerica.net/Lavender.htm. Accessed February 26, 2019.

"Daffodils: Beautiful but Potentially Toxic." Poison Control: National Capital Poison Center. https://www.poison.org/articles/2015-mar/daffodils. Accessed February 25, 2019.

Daniels, E. "History and Meaning of Calla Lilies." ProFlowers. https://www.proflowers.com/blog/calla-lily-meaning. Last modified January 15, 2019.

"Dante Gabriel Rossetti." The Metropolitan Museum of Art. https://www.metmuseum.org/art/collection/search/337500. Accessed February 28, 2019.

"Darwin-Hooker Letters." Cambridge Digital Library. https://cudl.lib.cam.ac.uk/collections/darwinhooker/1. Accessed March 1, 2019.

Darwin, C. "To Gardeners' Chronicle." University of Cambridge Darwin Correspondence project. https://www.darwinproject.ac.uk/letter/DCP-LETT-2826.xml. Accessed February 28, 2019.

Davis, C. "Sunflower Seeds and Oil." Colorado Integrated Food Safety Center of Excellence. https://fsi.colostate.edu/sunflower-seeds-draft/. Last modified 2017.

Dharmanada, S. "White Peony, Red Peony, and Moutan: Three Chinese Herbs Derived from *Paeonia*." Institute for Traditional Medicine. http://www.itmonline.org/arts/peony.htm. Accessed February 28, 2019.

"Dianthus 'Devon Xera' Fire Star." Missouri Botanical Garden. http://www.missouribotanicalgarden.org/PlantFinder/PlantFinderDetails.aspx?kempercode=d791. Accessed February 22, 2019.

"Diorissimo Christian Dior for Women." Fragrantica. fhttps://www.fragrantica.com/perfume/Christian-Dior/Diorissimo-224.html. Accessed February 27, 2019.

Doerflinger, F. "The Hyacinth Story." Old House Gardens. https://oldhousegardens.com/HyacinthHistory. Accessed February 26, 2019.

"Double Ninth Festival (Chongyang Festival)." Travel China Guide. https://www.travelchinaguide.com/essential/holidays/chongyang.htm. Last modified November 1, 2018.

"Early Bloomer: Ancient Sunflower Fossil Colors Picture of Eocene Flora." Scientific American. https://www.scientificamerican.com/gallery/early-bloomer-ancient-sunflower-fossil-colors-picture-of-eocene-flora/. Accessed March 1, 2019.

Edwards, M. and L. Abadie. "ZINNIAS FROM SPACE! NASA Studies the Multiple Benefits of Gardening." National Aeronautics and Space Administration. https://www.nasa.gov/content/ZINNIAS-FROM-SPACE-NASA-Studies-the-Multiple-Benefits-of-Gardening. Last modified August 16, 2016.

Evans, M. "Coco Chanel's Relationship with the Camellia." The Telegraph. https://www.telegraph.co.uk/gardening/how-to-grow/chanel-s-favourite-flower-the-camellia/. Last modified October 19, 2015.

———. "Memories of My Mother, Audrey Hepburn the Gardener." *The Telegraph*. https://www.telegraph.co.uk/gardening/gardens-to-visit/memories-of-my-mother-as-a-gardener-audrey-hepburn-by-luca-dotti/. Last modified September 15, 2015.

"Songs in T.S. Eliot's *The Waste Land*." Exploring *The Waste Land*. http://world.std.com/~raparker/exploring/thewasteland/exsongs.html. Accessed March 4, 2019.

"Floral Collars from Tutankhamun's Embalming Cache." The Metropolitain Museum of Art. https://www.metmuseum.org/toah/works-of-art/09.184.214-.216/. Accessed February 28, 2019.

"Flower Fields of the Netherlands." Netherlands Tourism. http://www.netherlands-tourism.com/flower-fields-netherlands/. Accessed February 25, 2019.

"Forget-Me-Not." The Flower Expert. https://www.theflowerexpert.com/content/growingflowers/flowersandseasons/forget-me-not. Accessed February 25, 2019.

"Foxglove." Cornell University Growing Guide. http://www.gardening.cornell.edu/homegardening/scenec1a6.html. Accessed February 25, 2019.

"Foxglove." WebMD. https://www.webmd.com/vitamins/ai/ingredientmono-287/foxglove. Accessed February 25, 2019.

"Fuchsia." Missouri Botanical Garden. http://www.missouribotanicalgarden.org/PlantFinder/PlantFinderDetails.aspx?kempercode=a511. Accessed February 25, 2019.

"Fuzhou Jasmine and Tea Culture System."
Food and Agriculture Organization of the
United Nations. http://www.fao.org/giahs
/giahsaroundtheworld/designated-sites
/asia-and-the-pacific/fuzhou-jasmine
-and-tea-culture-system/en/. Accessed
February 26, 2019.

"Georgia O'Keeffe: Visions of Hawai'i." New
York Botanical Garden. https://www.nybg
.org/event/georgia-okeeffe-visions-hawaii/.
Accessed February 26, 2019.

Gutowski, L. D. "Tulips Once Cost a
Man's Fortune." *New York Times*. https://
www.nytimes.com/1979/10/28/archives
/tulips-once-cost-a-mans-fortune
-tulipomania.html. Last modified
October 28, 1979.

Harkup, Ka. "It Was All Yellow: Did Digitalis
Affect the Way Van Gogh Saw the World?"
The Guardian. https://www.theguardian.com
/science/blog/2017/aug/10/it-was-all-yellow
-did-digitalis-affect-the-way-van-gogh-saw
-the-world. Last modified August 10, 2017.

Hass, N. "Francis Kurkdjian and Fabien
Ducher, Changing History in a Bottle."
New York Times Style Magazine.
https://www.nytimes.com/2015/09/24
/t-magazine/francis-kurkdjian-fabien
-ducher-rose.html. Last modified
September 24, 2015.

Heigl, A. "Remembering Anna Jarvis, the
Woman Behind Mother's Day." *People*.
https://people.com/human-interest
/mothers-day-founder-anna-jarvis/.
Last modified May 14, 2017.

"Hero to Leander." Perseus Digital Library.
http://www.perseus.tufts.edu/hopper
/text?doc=Ov.%20Ep.%2018&lang=original.
Accessed February 28, 2019.

"Hibiscus Trionum." Missouri
Botanical Garden. http://www
.missouribotanicalgarden.org
/PlantFinder/PlantFinderDetails
.aspx?kempercode=b943. Accessed
February 26, 2019.

Hirsch, M. L. "Where to See Thousands
and Thousands of Tulips." Smithsonian.com.
https://www.smithsonianmag.com/travel
/where-catch-tulip-mania-180954717/?page=6.
Last modified May 13, 2016.

"History." The National Sunflower Association.
shttps://www.sunflowernsa.com/all-about
/history/. Accessed March 1, 2019.

"History of Fuchsias." The British Fuchsia
Society. https://www.thebfs.org.uk
/historyoffuchsias.asp. Accessed
February 25, 2019.

Hobbs, H. "Preservation Group Discovers
Fairfax County's Past as It Cleans Up Graves."
Washington Post. https://www.washingtonpost
.com/local/preservation-group
-discovers-fairfax-countys-past-as-it
-cleans-up-graves/2012/11/20/74e6f268
-314d-11e2-9f50-0308e1e75445_story.html
?utm_term=.8147335a4f6b. Last modified
November 20, 2012.

Hone, D. "Moth Tongues, Orchids and
Darwin—The Predictive Power of Evolution.
The Guardian. thttps://www
.theguardian.com/science/lost-worlds/2013
/oct/02/moth-tongues-orchids-darwin
-evolution. Last modified October 2, 2013.

Horsbrugh, B. "The Hellespont Swim:
Following in Byron's Wake." *The Guardian*.
https://www.theguardian.com
/lifeandstyle/2010/may/06/hellespont-swim
-byron. Last modified May 6, 2010.

Hosch, W. L. "Gillyflower." *Encylopaedia
Britannica*. bhttps://www.britannica.com
/plant/gillyflower. Last modified June 26, 2008.

Howard, J. "The Flowers of Ancient Egypt
and Today." Tour Egypt. http://www
.touregypt.net/featurestories/flowers.htm.
Accessed February 25, 2019.

Huber, K. "Cheerful Marigold Is Flower of
the Dead." *Houston Chronicle*. https://www
.chron.com/life/article/Cheerful-marigold
-is-flower-of-the-dead-2245436.php. Last
modified October 31, 2011.

"Hyacinthoides Hispanica." Missouri
Botanical Garden. http://www
.missouribotanicalgarden.org/PlantFinder
/PlantFinderDetails.aspx?kempercode
=q740. Accessed February 26, 2019.

"Hyacinthus: Greek Mythology." *Encyclopedia
Britannica*. https://www.britannica.com
/topic/Hyacinthus. Accessed February 26, 2019.

"Hyacinthus Orientalis." Missouri
Botanical Garden. http://www
.missouribotanicalgarden.org/PlantFinder
/PlantFinderDetails.aspx?kempercode
=a458. Accessed February 26, 2019.

"Hydrangea." WebMD. https://www.webmd
.com/vitamins/ai/ingredientmono-663
/hydrangea. Accessed February 26, 2019.

"Hydrangea Flower Facts to Ring in the Season."
Calyx Flowers. https://www.calyxflowers
.com/blog/hydrangea-flower-facts-ring
-season/. Accessed February 26, 2019.

"Hydrangea Macrophylla." Missouri
Botanical Garden. http://www
.missouribotanicalgarden.org/PlantFinder
/PlantFinderDetails.aspx?taxonid=265518.
Accessed February 26, 2019.

"Iris." Theoi Greek Mythology. https://www
.theoi.com/Pontios/Iris.html. Accessed
February 26, 2019.

"Iris Pseudacorus." University of Florida
Institute of Food and Agricultural Sciences.
https://plants.ifas.ufl.edu/plant
-directory/iris-pseudacorus/. Accessed
February 26, 2019.

Jie, Ma Wen. "Flowers Native to Egypt."
Garden Guides. https://www.gardenguides
.com/116924-flowers-native-egypt.html. Last
modified September 21, 2017.

"June: Peony." Santa Fe Botanical Garden.
https://santafebotanicalgarden.org/june
-2012/. Accessed February 28, 2019.

Kegan, K. "The History of the Lily: The Pure
Flower." Blossom Flower Shops. https://
www.blossomflower.com/blog/history-lily
-pure-flower/. Last modified May 19, 2014.

Keil, D. "Carduus Linnaeus." Flora of
North America. http://www.efloras
.org/florataxon.aspx?flora_id=1&taxon
_id=105640. Accessed March 1, 2019.

Kelleher, K. "Fuchsia, The Pinky Purple of
Victorian Gardens and 'Miami Vice.'" The
Awl. https://www.theawl.com/2017/12
/fuchsia-the-pinky-purple-of-victorian
-gardens-and-miami-vice/. Last modified
December 5, 2017.

Kelley, J. "You Can Use That Rose Geranium
Plant for Cooking Too." *Los Angeles Times*.
https://www.latimes.com/food/dailydish
/la-fo-rose-geranium-recipes-20170314
-story.html. Last modified April 20, 2017.

Kennedy, Merrit. "The Mystery of Why
Sunflowers Follow the Sun—Solved."
NPR. https://www.npr.org/sections
/thetwo-way/2016/08/05/488891151/the
-mystery-of-why-sunflowers-turn-to
-follow-the-sun-solved. Last modified
August 5, 2016.

Larkin, D. "When This You See, Remember
Me." The Metropolitan Museum of Art,
The Cloisters Museum & Gardens.
http://blog.metmuseum.org
/cloistersgardens/2013/05/10
/when-this-you-see-remember-me
/#more-10480. Last modified May 10, 2013.

"Lavandula Angustifolia 'Hidcote.'"
Missouri Botanical Garden. http://www
.missouribotanicalgarden.org/PlantFinder
/PlantFinderDetails.aspx?kempercode
=q830. Accessed February 26, 2019.

"Le Magnolia de la Maillardére." Jardins Nantes.
https://jardins.nantes.fr/N/Plante
/Collection/Magnolia/Histoire-Magnolia
-Maillardiere.asp. Accessed March 4, 2019.

"Leiden Botanic Garden Design." The
Garden Guide. https://www.gardenvisit
.com/book/history_of_garden
_design_and_gardening/chapter_3
_european_gardens_(500ad-1850)
/leiden_botanic_garden_design. Accessed
February 26, 2019.

"Leonhart Fuchs." Iowa State University:
The Three Founders of Botany. http://
historicexhibits.lib.iastate.edu/botanists
/leonhart_fuchs.html. Accessed
February 25, 2019.

Liberman, A. "Etymologists at War with a
Flower: Foxglove." Oxford University Press's
Academic Insights for the Thinking World:
OUPblog. https://blog.oup.com/2010/11/
foxglove/. Last modified November 10, 2010.

Liu, P.-L., Q. Wan, Y.-P. Guo, et al. "Phylogeny
of the Genus Chrysanthemum L.:
Evidence from Single-Copy Nuclear Gene
and Chloroplast DNA Sequences." Plus One.
https://journals.plos.org/plosone
/article?id=10.1371/journal.pone.0048970. Last
modified November 1, 2012.

"Lilacs at the Arnold Arboretum." The Arnold
Arboretum of Harvard University. https://
www.arboretum.harvard.edu
/plants/featured-plants/lilacs/plants-of
-history-plants-for-tomorrow/. Accessed
February 26, 2019.

Lisina, E. "Bunkyo Azalea Festival: Annual
Festival of Azalea at Nezu Shrine." Japan Travel.
https://en.japantravel.com/tokyo/bunkyo
-azalea-festival/37423. Last modified May 1, 2017.

"Lord Byron Swims the Hellespont." History.
com. https://www.history.com/this-day-in
-history/lord-byron-swims-the-hellespont.
Last modified November 13, 2009.

Luna, R. "Edible Flowers and Plants You Can
Find in Mexico and How to Prepare Them."
Matador Network. https://matadornetwork
.com/bnt/edible-flowers-plants-can-find
-mexico-prepare/. Last modified June 1, 2015.

"Manuscripts and Special Collections:
Measurements." The University of
Nottingham. https://www.nottingham.ac.uk
/manuscriptsandspecialcollections
/researchguidance/weightsandmeasures
/measurements.aspx. Accessed March 1, 2019.

"Marigold Marks Day of the Dead." *Daily Herald*
online. https://www.dailyherald.com/article
/20101029/entlife/710319991/. Last modified
October 29, 2010.

Martens, J. A. "Blue Peonies." DIY Network.
https://www.diynetwork.com/how-to
/outdoors/gardening/blue-peonies. Accessed
March 1, 2019.

"Medieval Sourcebook: Nizami (1140-1203 CE): Khosru & Shireen, c. 1190)." Fordham University. shttps://sourcebooks.fordham .edu/source/1190nizami1.asp. Accessed March 1, 2019.

Morton, H. "Mission and History of the North Carolina Azalea Festival." North Carolina Azalea Festival. https://ncazaleafestival .org/about-us/mission-history/. Accessed February 22, 2019.

Meyers, R. L. and H. C. Minor. "Sunflower: An American Native." Extension University of Missouri. ehttps://extension2.missouri.edu /g4290. Last modified October 1993.

"Myosotis Sylvatica." Missouri Botanical Garden. http://www. missouribotanicalgarden.org/PlantFinder /PlantFinderDetails.aspx?taxonid=278005. Accessed February 25, 2019.

Nelson, Jennifer Schultz. "Zinnias." University of Illinois Extension. https://web.extension. illinois.edu/dmp/palette/080601.html. Last modified June 1, 2008.

Newman, Joyce. "Darwin's Star Orchid." New York Botanical Garden. https://www.nybg .org/blogs/plant-talk/2012/03/exhibit-news /darwins-garden/darwins-star-orchid/. Last modified March 29, 2012.

Nicole. "Texas Wedding at Honey Creek Ranch." Southern Weddings. https:// southernweddings.com/tag/snapdragon -bouquet/. Last modified August 14, 2012.

"Nyx." Theoi Greek Mythology. https://www .theoi.com/Protogenos/Nyx.html. Accessed February 28, 2019.

"Opium." U.S. National Library of Medicine. https://www.nlm.nih.gov/exhibition /pickyourpoison/exhibition-opium.html. Accessed February 28, 2019.

"Peony." Chicago Botanic Garden. https:// www.chicagobotanic.org/plantinfo/peony. Accessed February 28, 2019.

"Peony." Kaiser Permanente. https:// wa.kaiserpermanente.org/kbase/topic .jhtml?docId=hn-3658006. Accessed August 6, 2019.

"Peony—Plant of Healing." National Park Service. https://www.nps.gov/saga/learn /education/upload/Greek%20Myths -Flowers.pdf. Accessed February 28, 2019.

"Periwinkle Initiative." The Colonial Williamsburg Foundation. http://slaveryandremembrance .org/partners/partncr/?id=P0087. Accessed February 28, 2019.

"Persian Lily." Lurie Garden. https://www .luriegarden.org/plants/persian-lily/. Accessed February 27, 2019.

Petruzzello, M. "Prunus." Encyclopaedia Britannica. https://www.britannica.com /plant/Prunus. Last modified January 28, 2015.

Phippard, J. "Stopping to Smell the Rhododendron." The Rockefeller University. http://selections.rockefeller.edu /stopping-to-smell-the-rhododendron/. Last modified June 13, 2013.

"Poppy." American Legion Auxiliary. https:// www.alaforveterans.org/Poppy/. Accessed February 28, 2019.

"Ranunculaceae." Botanical Dermatology Database. https://www.botanical -dermatology-database.info/BotDermFolder/ RANU.html#Ranunculus. Last modified January 2013.

"Renoir Landscapes." The Philadelphia Museum of Art. https://www.philamuseum .org/booklets/2_11_26_1.html. Accessed February 25, 2019.

"Robinia Pseudoacacia." Missouri Botanical Garden. http://www. missouribotanicalgarden.org/PlantFinder /PlantFinderDetails.aspx?kempercode =c143. Accessed March 1, 2019.

"Robinia Pseudoacacia (Black Locust)." CABI Invasive Species Compendium. https://www .cabi.org/isc/datasheet/47698. Last modified November 8, 2018.

"Rose Folklore." Rose Magazine. http:// www.rosemagazine.com/articles07/rose _folklore/. Accessed March 1, 2019.

Rose, S. "The Great British Tea Heist." Smithsonian.com. shttps://www .smithsonianmag.com/history/the -great-british-tea-heist-9866709/. Last modified March 9, 2010.

Sampaolo, M. "Fleur-de-lis." *Encyclopaedia Britannica*. https://www.britannica.com /topic/fleur-de-lis. Last modified June 7, 2017.

Schreiber, H. "Curious Chemistry Guides Hydrangea Colors." *American Scientist*. https://www.americanscientist.org/article /curious-chemistry-guides-hydrangea -colors. Accessed February 26, 2019.

"'Seahenge' Early Bronze Age Timber Circle on Holme Beach." *Norfolk Heritage Explorer*. http://www.heritage.norfolk.gov.uk/record -details?MNF33771-%27Seahenge%27-Early -Bronze-Age-timber-circle-on-Holme-Beach &Index=2&RecordCount=1&SessionID=a2c4 013d-621a-4e17-86a9-009ca304ec34. Accessed February 26, 2019.

"Shakespeare Lives in Science: Poisons, Potions, and Drugs." Shakespeare Lives. https://www.shakespearelives.org/poisons-potions/. Accessed February 28, 2019.

Smith, A R. "Zinnia." Flora of North America. http://www.efloras.org/florataxon.aspx?flora_id=1&taxon_id=135326. Accessed March 1, 2019.

Studebaker, R. "In Our Gardens: Victorian Forcing Vases Will Produce Beautiful Hyacinths." Tulsa World. https://www.tulsaworld.com/archives/in-our-gardens-victorian-forcing-vases-will-produce-beautiful-hyacinths/article_c3bfa505-cc86-5f56-8a30-bceec445583a.html. Last modified January 21, 2006.

Takeda, E. "Significance of Sakura: Cherry Blossom Traditions in Japan." Smithsonian Institution. https://festival.si.edu/blog/2014/significance-of-sakura-cherry-blossom-traditions-in-japan/. Last modified April 9, 2014.

"The Double Ninth Festival." China Highlights. https://www.chinahighlights.com/festivals/the-double-ninth-festival.htm. Accessed February 25, 2019.

"The Most Ancient and Most Noble Order of the Thistle." The Encyclopedia Britannica. https://www.britannica.com/topic/The-Most-Ancient-and-Most-Noble-Order-of-the-Thistle. Last updated April 12, 2012.

"The Pansy." East London Garden Society. http://www.elgs.org.uk/pf-pansy.html. Accessed February 28, 2019.

"The Victorian Vision of China and Japan." Victoria and Albert Museum. http://www.vam.ac.uk/content/articles/t/the-victorian-vision-of-china-and-japan/. Accessed March 4, 2019.

Thompson, Sylvia. "Garden Fresh: Please Eat the Geraniums." *Los Angeles Times.* https://www.latimes.com/archives/la-xpm-1994-10-06-fo-46947-story.html. Last modified October 6, 1994.

Vallejo-Marin, M. "Revealed: The First Flower, 140-million Years Old, Looked Like a Magnolia." Scientific American. https://www.scientificamerican.com/article/revealed-the-first-flower-140-million-years-old-looked-like-a-magnolia/. Last modified August 1, 2017.

"Vanilla." New World Encyclopedia. nhttp://www.newworldencyclopedia.org/entry/Vanilla. Accessed February 28, 2019.

Vargues, L. "Flashes in the Twilight." New York Botanical Garden. https://www.nybg.org/blogs/science-talk/2013/12/flashes-in-the-twilight/. Last modified December 30, 2013.

Visser, M. "Homemade Honeysuckle Syrup and 6 Ways to Use It." The Herbal Academy. https://theherbalacademy.com/homemade-honeysuckle-syrup/. Last modified June 14, 2017.

Ward, R. "Ask Rufus: Gardens of 'Youth and Old Age.'" The Dispatch. https://www.cdispatch.com/opinions/article.asp?aid=34477. Last modified June 28, 2014.

"Waterlily House." Kew Royal Botanical Gardens. https://www.kew.org/kew-gardens/whats-in-the-gardens/waterlily-house. Accessed March 1, 2019.

"Why Buttercups Reflect Yellow on Chins." University of Cambridge. https://www.cam.ac.uk/research/news/why-buttercups-reflect-yellow-on-chins. Accessed February 22, 2019.

"Why Is a Specific Flower Offered to a Specific God?" Hindu Janajagruti Samiti .https://www.hindujagruti.org/hinduism/hinduism-practices/dev-puja/offering-flowers-to-god. Accessed February 26, 2019.

"Why the Green Carnation." Oscar Wilde Tours. https://www.oscarwildetours.com/about-our-symbol-the-green-carnation/. Accessed February 22, 2019.

"Wild Daisy." WebMD. https://www.webmd.com/vitamins/ai/ingredientmono-9/wild-daisy. Accessed February 25, 2019.

Woolf, M. "Oscar Wilde's Carnation Makes a Stately Return." *Independent.* https://www.independent.co.uk/news/uk/home-news/oscar-wildes-carnation-makes-a-stately-return-1589424.html. Last modified July 2, 1995.

Xiaoru, C. "Carving a Beautiful Bloom." *Global Times.* ghttp://www.globaltimes.cn/content/842053.shtml. Last modified February 12, 2014.

York, P. S. "The Real Trick to the Prettiest Peony Arrangement." *Southern Living.* https://www.southernliving.com/garden/flowers/peony-arrangement-tips. Accessed March 1, 2019.

Zhou, L. "Orchidelirium, and Obsession with Orchids, Has Lasted for Centuries." Smithsonian.com. https://www.smithsonianmag.com/smithsonian-institution/orchidelirium-obsession-orchids-lasted-centuries-180954060/. Last modified January 29, 2015.

THE LANGUAGE OF FLOWERS

HarperCollins books may be purchased for
educational, business, or sales promotional use.
For information, please email the Special Markets
Department at SPsales@harpercollins.com.

First published in 2020 by
Harper Design
An Imprint of HarperCollins*Publishers*
195 Broadway
New York, NY 10007
Tel: (212) 207-7000
Fax: (855) 746-6023
harperdesign@harpercollins.com
www.hc.com

Distributed throughout the world by
HarperCollins*Publishers*
195 Broadway
New York, NY 10007

ISBN 978-0-06-287319-4

Library of Congress Cataloging-in-Publication Data: 2018938728

Book design by Shubhani Sarkar and Odessa Begay

Printed in Malaysia

Second Printing, 2021

About the Author

Odessa Begay is the author of the adult coloring books *Little Birds*, *Edgar Allan Poe*, *Jingle Bells Christmas Carol*, and *William Shakespeare*. A graduate of New York University's Tisch School of the Arts, she illustrates full-time for an array of clients, which have included Papyrus, Design Design, and Robin Sprong Wallpaper. She lives in Kansas City with her husband and dog, Archie. Odessabegay.com.